Life LIGHT

THE PURSUIT OF YOUR BEST SELF

AYANA THOMAS

For permission requests and more information, write to the author at foryoulibertywrites@gmail.com.

Liberty Writes
Washington, DC
Printed in the United States of America

ISBN: 978-0-578-61042-9

Liberty Writes

COMMITMENT TO READERS

I want every word that I write to bring readers to a place of liberty – free from the concerns of this world, free from the cares of life, and free from self-destruction.

The bottom line is – I want you to be free.

The passion behind *Life Light* stems from experiences that have refined me. There is a famous saying that "experience is the best teacher". My perspective is that shared experience is the bridge to greatness. Equipped with the knowledge of shared experience, we can be strategic about the steps that we take to walk into our purpose.

Life Light developed out of several transitional experiences that allowed me to think broader, vibe higher, and love deeper.

I invite you on this journey with me and I am hopeful that you will benefit from my experiences. Let these lessons catapult you into
your now and next.

Peace and Liberty!

Ayana

A Forward Like No Other

At my core, I am a teacher. I have to give some instructions before you read this book (and yes, there will be homework)!

You are not required to read *Life Light* in sequential order. Live a little! Read according to which areas of your life, need the most light (and work).

Have fun with *Life Light*! This whole set up may feel very formal. Just know that I have GREAT disdain for formality. So do not make a big deal out of this forward or the asks therein. These tips are here to help you have a great experience with *Life Light*. When you are reading and working through the book, I hope you feel an easiness - maybe even stress and burdens lifting off you as you read.

Life Light is not intended to be gospel, represent scientific facts, or historic truths - it is experiential. My experiences - lived out loud for all to see and grow from. You may completely agree with my thought flow and in other instances, you may not. That is ok. Let's learn how to abide in difference together.

Life Light includes 13 chapters and 13 short reflections. The chapters and the reflections may have some connecting themes, but they are not intended to be paired together to the point that they cannot stand on their own.

I love words - that's all. Period. Point blank. I believe that there are fundamental tools in the etymology of a word. So put your definition seat belt on, and take this word journey with me. No eye rolling allowed.

This is not a speed-read friends. Take your speedreaders off. Do not shortchange yourself by speeding through just to check the box at the end of each chapter. Read for meaning, alignment, and for deeper purpose.

Make sure you have a pen and highlighter when you read, so that you can take notes. If you are reading the ebook - learn how to use those features through the app or device, you are using.

If you read something and have no idea what I am talking about, break out your dictionary or google it. This is a judgement free classroom. I want you to learn for life application sake, so do what you need to do to get there.

There are a number of intersections in the focus areas of the book. Many of the focus areas are interdependent. I have taken strides to call out those connections so that you can find the references easily. The callouts will look like this (Perspective, p. 31)

The chapters are brief, but thought provoking (hopefully paradigm shifting for you). Sometimes, I think authors say too much and dilute their points. Not here. I have included what was important. Thoughts that did not fit were extracted or will be included in my future books.

Last thing…please do not keep this light to yourself. Share this goodness with others - buy copies for your neighbors, family, friends, co-workers, and community members.

We all need a little light - don't forget to keep yours on.

Liberty Writes
24 Second Rule™

The pen is a reflection prompt. I have inserted these prompts in various locations throughout the book to help you practice intentional reflection. There are probing questions and thoughts in this book that will require you to take a break from reading and be present with your thoughts and feelings before you move forward.

Please honor the reflection prompt. When you get to a prompt, please put the book down and think. It is important for you to focus your thoughts and listen to your inner voice. Some thoughts might be intimidating initially. Do not let that deter you. When you have made the necessary discoveries and come to the necessary conclusions, take some notes and read on!

Reflection Pro-Tip: At a minimum, use the reflection prompt to practice the **Liberty Writes 24 Second Rule.** Close your eyes and take three deep breaths. This should take you about 24 seconds to complete. These deep breaths help to center you and give you a break from the racing thoughts in your mind. At some reflection prompts, that will be all that you need.

Happy Reflecting!

BOOK 1
Knowing

- Consistently Lit
- Journey/Evolution
- Mindwholeness
- Knowledge and Learning
- Perspective
- Trauma

REFLECTIONS:

- Your Role in Vision
- Stay in the Now
- Manifest
- On Words...

BOOK 2
Being

- Connectedness
- Love
- Children

REFLECTIONS:

- Identity
- Reputation
- O.Y.S.
- Ask for Help

BOOK 3
Becoming

- Freedom
- Peace
- Grace
- Purpose

REFLECTIONS:

- The Power of Choice
- Cultivating
- Stewardship
- Know Your Worth
- Clarity

BONUS
Section

- Liberty Writes Word Bank
- Revolutionary Reads
- Thomas Model of Individual Learning
- Thomas Model on Teacher /Student Duality
- Works Cited/ Referenced
- Meet the Author & Liberty Writes

BOOK 1
Knowing

Consistently Lit

As a child, I remember asking my parents to leave the light on in my dad's closet every night as they tucked me into bed. There was something about having the light on that made me feel safe enough to put my trust in sleep; to believe that I would be safe throughout the night and more importantly that I would wake up again when the sun took its position in the sky the next morning. I vividly remember the feeling of comfort, knowing that with the light on, I was strong enough to be alone. The small light shining from the crack in the door made me feel invincible and untouchable. If all else failed, with the light shining, I could at least see if some horrible evil monster was coming to eat me in the middle of the night. The light reassured me, quieted my spirit, and soothed my soul - night after night.

As an adult, I grew out of the practice of keeping a light on. Now, I thrive in cool, dark spaces with minimal light. Maybe it is the introvert in me, but I feel like I can fully relax when the room is dark. Being – in the dark forces me to transition my focus from the racing thoughts in my mind to the stillness around me. Darkness feels very personal and soothing to me (my truth - maybe not yours). Bright lights are just downright offensive to me. There are times when the light feels like an abrupt and unwelcome disruption. In these moments, I try to block out the light like a frantic sailor trying to plug up a hole in a sinking ship. I have tried to control the amount of light I allow in my space. I like darkness so much that I purchased room-darkening blinds, dark bedding for my bed, and an eyeshade to make sure the light does not kill my vibe. What I found though, is that even in an environment intentionally designed for darkness, there is always a light that pushes through. Whether it is the light from the cable box, the light from the streetlights outside, or the moonlight, there is always light present to infiltrate my planned darkness.

Then my kid comes along and I am not exactly sure who put her on to the game, but now, she refuses to fall asleep in the dark. It's a thing. Do not try to turn the light off before she is good and asleep. Oh no. That triggers World War III in the form of late night sobs, full body temper tantrums, and maximum bouts of drama. To avoid the war on drama, the light stays on and then all is right in her world. I turn her closet light on and then roll my eyes as I walk out of her room. She wins again – EYE ROLL.

I thought I had done a good job raising her to be a strong, independent woman of the millennium, who thrives in darkness also. Despite my best efforts, she feels that same comforting reassurance that I felt as a child when the light was on at night. The light gives her a sense of peace and encourages her to be independent in a way that daylight alone, cannot. Reliving my experiences as a child and now seeing this same behavior in my child has reaffirmed for me that no matter how hard you work to stay in a dark place - the light always wins.

On New Year's Eve, when people are out sipping champagne and celebrating the start of a new year, I purpose that time to sit quietly, listen for direction, and develop my goals for the year ahead. Not long ago, the direction that I received was "to be a light in the world". Ok - piece of cake, right? NO! BIG NO! What does that even mean? Be a light in the world? (The world, Craig! Not just the city, but the world! They need light in the world, Craig! - this is an inside movie joke if you have no idea what I am talking about). The responsibility frightened me. I took a few notes to capture the direction and walked away from it.

It was a little over a year before I understood what this direction really meant. I was explaining my book concept to a friend and the original title that I was using did not connect at all with the overall purpose of the book. My poor friend was trying to be as supportive as possible, but I could see the confusion on her face. As I was driving, the idea to call the book *Life Light* just dropped in my lap. As I meditated on the name for the book, the light turned on for me and suddenly everything made sense. It is my assignment to be the metaphoric light for others - hopefully you reading this book. My work will provide that same sense of comfort and empowerment to others that the closet light gave me as a child. I am hopeful that *Life Light* will shine a light for you with the turn of every page. The chapters and reflections will help you follow the light in pursuit of your best self. More importantly, I am hopeful that you will now understand the benefit of keeping the light on for yourself and for others that you will teach or mentor in the future.

Think about times when you've been in a completely dark place trying to find a light switch to turn on. Many people are in that space in life - trying to work their way across a room of undefined obstacles just to have a little light bring clarity to everything. In order to keep the light on, you have to do something. Action or assembly will be required. There are many ways that we take action to keep the light on.

For example, lighting a candle requires some level of skill, especially if you do not have one of those fancy, extended candle lighters. If you are in a dark room, you have to turn on a light switch or get up to open the blinds. There it is - the required effort on your part to initiate or maintain the light in your life.

As I bring this chapter to a close, there were a few things that stood out to me about light, that I think are worth sharing briefly:

BEING ABLE TO SEE

Light enhances the ability to see; see what is immediately in front of you, behind you, and around you. More importantly, light gives you the ability to see beyond you, as far as vision will take you. My brother and I were joking about the scene in The Lion King where Mufasa explains to Simba that everything the light touches is part of their kingdom. The truth that the king shares in this moment is too broad for the young heir to grasp. Mufasa tries to covey to his son that his realm is boundless. Boundless, friends.

Being able to see is serious business. Like Simba, we have to be able to perceive the same limitless possibilities in our lives. Our humanity will only allow us to go as far as we can see, before fear sets in and our pace slows (sometimes to a screeching halt). There will be times when you will have to proceed into some darkness to reach purpose. Your ability to maintain clear vision will have a profound impact on your long-term success.

KEEPING THE LIGHT ON

Every day that you live, something or someone will come along to try to steal your shine. I intentionally selected the lessons outlined in the book, to help you keep your light on, as you pursue your best self. You may have to light sage to ward off evil spirits, or block relatives/friends with toxic energy, or you may have to avoid certain places or people to stay lit. Keeping the light on is more than a figure of speech - action is consistently required for you to keep the light on.

BEING LIGHT FOR OTHERS

We have to be in tune with the needs of others - those in our close circle and those we do not even know. You never know how acknowledging someone, a total stranger, can help them to feel seen, relevant, and necessary in this world.

Don't you know what it's like to feel like all hope is lost and then someone comes along and acknowledges you? It's like the dam opens up and all of that water washes away anything that may have been troubling you. We have the power to be light for someone else - to reassure them that things will get better or to encourage them to walk boldly through some life circumstance that is challenging them. Just by being present - you can help someone to feel safe, protected, and cared for. Also, your presence as light, can help others to see.

We are all in this together. Let us light the way forward!

Journey/Evolution

"Don't worry about what to do with your life, create the life you want."
- Unknown

There is so much direction and meaning in this quote - such a vibe. The quote suggests that it is more important to focus your energy on actively working towards the life you want, than it is to be stuck focusing on perfecting the master plan for your life. Do you know what you want? Are you open to the reality that what you want might change? What I wanted for myself 10 years ago, 5 years ago, or heck even three months ago has changed as I have evolved and as life has evolved around me. Life is a journey - the path beyond the horizon, unseen. The unseen and the unknown can cause great intimidation, if we are not open to following the divine order for evolution and growth in our lives.

From my perspective (and pen), to evolve is to follow the free flow of development over time, as you learn from and interact with yourself, your tribe, and the world around you. The key, in my interpretation of the definition of evolve, is to follow. So many times we trick ourselves by thinking that we are in control. Having the discipline to follow is mastering (self) control.

When I think about evolution, I think about Metamorphosis by Frank Kafka. For some reason, this story spoke to me as a high school student, reading it for the first time. I identified with Gregor's plight as he was on an unexpected path that his family could not comprehend and refused to support. Evolution for Gregor, like many of us, was uncomfortable, unclear, and was a path that he unfortunately had to follow alone. In the story, he changes into a completely different life form. All of a sudden, he doesn't fit in because his path in life, made him new. Rather than taking advantage of the opportunity to embrace Gregor's diversity and abide in difference together (refer to *Life Light: The Workbook* for reflection), his family starved him and his purpose to death. Literally. Are you starving yourself (your evolution, your journey, etc.) to death trying to cling onto a reality that is not yours? Evolution is trying to push you forward into something greater!

I wonder where the school of thought came from, that requires 18-year-old child-adults, to know what they want to do when they graduate high school and head to college, trade school, or straight into a full time profession. Many full-grown adults are not quite sure what they want to do when they actually grow up. In many instances, WE (the full-grown adults just referenced) are also the ones working 60+ hours a week in a career not aligned with our purpose because it is what someone told us to do and not necessarily, what we should be doing. (This is not a dig - simply a fact. However, if you felt that personally, maybe now you will be motivated to stop chasing someone else's dream and go after yours. I digress... the work of a teacher is never ending...sigh). We have to stop reinforcing the behaviors and philosophies that teach us that there is only one way, the "right" way to do a thing. We will not all follow the same path. It is important though, that you are at least aware enough to know when a shift in the path is approaching so that you can adjust accordingly. Let's move on.

I am a linear thinker - learning to be comfortable in the abstract nature and ambiguity of life. This is not easy though - let me tell you. I was definitely raised to believe there was a natural order to how things were supposed to go. Somewhere along the way, in the people dynamics that I saw in my Cleveland Heights neighborhood, the great family oriented television shows of the late 80's/early 90's, and the examples in my family taught me to believe that a successful life consisted of: high school/college, job, wedding, kid(s), and retire (in that order and nothing else lol). So I followed what I thought was the natural path for my life.

I left home for college at 18, just knowing that I was going away to become the world's greatest accountant. When I left for college, I had been working for my dad's business for 9 years (I officially earned my first paycheck at the age of 9). I thought that since I loved helping him keep the books, that I should totally be an accountant. I found the perfect degree program, at the perfect college, at a perfect distance away from my parents. First day of class, Calculus 3…I walked out of class after 15 minutes. I was not interested in doing math on such an advanced level - who would be? In this moment of decision, it was almost like the ground shifted below me and a light encouraged me to follow a different extension of the path. I had to reconcile the reality that the path that I thought I was supposed to be on, was not my intended path. More importantly, my path was not as perfect as I had thought it would be. Oh well! On to the next one!

If I wasn't going to be an accountant, I wanted to at least find a way to help my family pay for my college education. So I signed up for Army ROTC. 4 years of in-school participation and 4 years of active duty after college, sounded like a piece of cake in exchange for thousands of dollars in tuition funding. I should have known when I had to be up, dressed, coherent, and halfway across campus by 6 a.m. that ROTC probably wasn't my vibe, but I made a commitment that I had to see through. First day of my PT class. I got up (way earlier than normal) and got myself together. I arrived at my first PT Class at 6:05 a.m. (5 minutes late) in a sleeveless, Tommy Hilfiger sundress and wedge flip flops (I remember this moment vividly lol). I walked in the armory and it was like time stood still. Everyone stared, pointed, and whispered about this silly girl arriving late and wearing a sundress. Yikes. Somehow everyone else in the class got the message that PT required tennis shoes and army fatigue pants. Have you ever tried hiking in a sundress and flip-flops in August? This was probably the most bizarre series of circumstances ever. I completed the morning hike, but left the gym as soon as we came back inside. NEVER to return. Just like that, my army career was over in less than an hour. Once again, the ground shifted below me and I realized that this was clearly not the right path for me.

What I appreciate about me, is that I have not been afraid to try different things to find the right fit for me. I changed my major 4 times between freshman and senior year. Each time, I got closer and closer to purpose. My path was not perfect, but had I not pursued what felt honest and true for me, I may not have had a successful and fulfilling college experience. What's worse, I would be miserable in a career and profession that I was not designed for.

Even to this day, close to 20 years later, I still don't know exactly what I want to be when I grow up. Writing this book and sharing these experiences with all of you lovely people feels like I am getting close. I don't want to jinx anything though, so I will just follow the flow and celebrate milestones along the way. I don't see not knowing exactly what I want to be when I grow up as me having a lack of focus or productivity. Some people cannot fathom how a person can have uncertainty about their life. I feel sorry for those people that have it all together. They never get to experience the true fluidity of life.

I see not knowing what I want to be when I grow up as following the journey designed for me. I want us to stop teaching children and adults that there is a "right way" to attain success. Sure there are many things that we should want the people in our lives to accomplish. At the same time, we have to be willing to give grace (Grace, p. 97) and allow people the space to find their way. Letting go of the need to control someone else's life is very liberating for you and for that person. It is hard for the people trying to live up to your expectations. Don't apply pressure unnecessarily. Exercise patience. The people you care about most will get there, in time.

Living in your personal truth is crucial. This is a lesson that I am learning how to apply and walk in. When you are honest with yourself and others, you are open to evolve. Evolution is required for completing the journey of life. Along the journey, you will encounter many different types of people – some that do not have your best interest at heart. Purpose leeches are people that are committed to sucking you dry of your purpose (Purpose, p. 103). They don't see the value in evolution and they don't want you to change/develop into all that you were created to become. You can identify a purpose leech when you hear one or all of these key phrases: "there is a right way to do something", "do what you were taught", or "this is the way it has always been done". If you hear someone use any of these three phrases, RUN. These people are not open to the power of evolution. They do not welcome change. Having them in your circle or your ear, can stifle your growth and delay your destiny. Do you have purpose leeches in your life? Purpose leech thinking is flawed and detrimental to you reaching and living in your full potential. RUN, friend, RUN!

I am not immune to advice from others, but I have always been clear about not accepting feedback that was not in agreement with who I am. Don't get me wrong, I am not suggesting that people in roles to influence others through wisdom (mentors, parents, teachers, etc.) should sit by idly and ignore someone important to them falling by the wayside. I am merely suggesting that there have to be boundaries around that influence to allow space for people to blossom naturally, overtime. There was a period in my life when one of my mentors told me, "I can't help you anymore, because you have surpassed my level of experience". Initially, this feedback hurt me to my core. I didn't quite understand what they were telling me. I felt abandoned and disappointed. I reflected on what my mentor told me, and in time I came to develop mad respect for them being self-aware enough and caring about me enough to step back, so as to not suppress my growth.

Many times, those of us with influence try to stay out front too long and end up derailing the path for those that are coming behind us. Worse, we project our fears, failures, or other insecurities onto those we are trying to help. Stop that! Get out of the leader seat and let people be great - in their own way. Celebrate their successes. Applaud their wins - even if you have to clap from the sideline. They are counting on you to be present, to encourage their growth (even in defeat), and stand by their side.

Life comes at you hard. Things that you never expected would happen to you, happen (especially if you only believe what you were taught). All of a sudden you are faced with a choice - do you rise to the occasion to meet the challenge or do you fall victim to your circumstances? I refuse to play the victim. I choose to rise! So I have had to remain extremely agile and patient with myself. I welcome the ups and downs of the journey. I welcome growth and am hungry for change. I am so proud of who I have become and even more excited to see who I will be when I reach my final sunset.

Peace.

Mindwholeness

24 hours a day, 7 days a week your brain is gathering, assessing, filtering, and grouping information. Even when you are sleeping, your brain regulates your body and keeps it operating normally. Essentially, the brain takes in so much information on a regular basis that it decides for you, what information is relevant enough to rise to the level of your conscious mind. Going further, the brain decides what information is useful enough to become a memory. Let that soak in. You think you're doing all of these amazing things on your own. You are not. Your brain is the master of everything that is you. Your mind needs to be whole.

WHAT IS MINDFULNESS?
The term mindfulness was originated by Buddhist scholar T.W. Rhys Davids in the late 1880's. A term largely unknown to many non-Buddhists, has recently become a trending topic over 100 years later in Western culture. This reality deserves a pause.

Don't ever think that the goodness you have is not for the world. This man, Mr. Davids, developed a concept over 100 years ago, that is just now taking the world by storm. You may not see your ideas take off the way you would like right away, but don't hold back your goodness for fear that someone won't understand. Put that ish out there and change the world - even if the world doesn't catch on for 100+ years.

Ok, back to mindfulness. Maybe you've known about it all of your life, but no one told me. That's the whole point of this book. We are vibing together about things that no one had the decency to share with the kid. At any rate, if you've never heard of the term or if you don't know much about it, that's great. Let's learn together.

Mindfulness, in the simplicity of its original definition means thought. The western adaptation of the word has furthered the definition to include: on purposeful and present thought. Today, right here, right now, I am furthering the definition of the word to include: present awareness of self, others, and the around (that is anything and everything around you). For so many reasons, there is a necessity for you to be present and aware of yourself, others, and what may be happening around you (Stay In The Now, p. 49).

So being the great mom that I am, I am trying to teach the concept of mindfulness to my kid (you will hear about her quite a bit - she is my muse). I think it is important for her to be mindful of herself, others, and especially the around. We live in dangerous times and I want her to know that staring down at a phone screen while she is walking across the street is not being mindful (or safe). As a child, she has a level of naiveté and innocence that does not register the significance of paying attention at all times. I understand that she is a child, so I do try to protect that safe space as much as I can.

However, when God blessed this earth with her presence, I committed to raising "smart kids in these streets". It is important to me that she has a heightened level of awareness so that she can navigate life independently, even as a child.

To help prepare her, I will make her stand still, close her eyes, and tell me what she observes when we are out on the town. There is a belief (maybe even a scientific fact) that when one sense is limited the other senses strengthen. When she is not depending on what she can see, she has to rely on what she can hear, feel, and smell. This is my way of teaching her to always be present in the moment. More importantly, to always pay attention to what is happening around her. These moments of awakening for her is how I see the definition of mindfulness coming to life.

Even with everything that mindfulness is, I don't think that is enough. So I am coining the term MINDWHOLENESS ™. I googled it and no one has claimed it yet. As far as I can tell, I'm the realist that's ever done it. Mindwholeness is the idea that the mind must be whole in order for you to have a proper relationship with yourself, others, and the around. Wholeness is the state of being complete and unbroken.

Many of us do not have whole minds and therefore our ability to practice mindfulness can be interrupted or impossible. We need to be sensitive to the fact that many of us are in this place for one reason or another. For those of us living with learning disabilities or mental illness, the struggle to be present and aware can be tough. For others, being mindful can be difficult when you are recovering from trauma or other life experiences that may be disorienting. Our minds just can't get right. In general, it is important that we are sensitive to the needs of others. We never know what someone may have survived or may be going through that is keeping them from being all that they can be. Be patient and be willing to be mindwhole with others.

Let's slow walk this together. We all know there are so many things that impact mental function. One of my favorite topics in my master's program was the concept of memory making. The experiences of your life form your mental memory -

good, bad, or ugly (Perspective, p. 31). Regardless of the condition of your mind, there are things that you can do to guard your mind. Remember it is through your mind that memories are made. It is through your mind that perspective is created. It is your mind, which dictates your behavior and your ability to achieve true mindfulness. To further the discussion, I have described categories of external stimuli that affect the mind. By understanding these mind encounters, you can take the steps necessary to protect your mind and reach mindwholeness.

DISORIENTATION

Disorientation is actually a great tool in learning. We usually associate disorientation with someone who is confused, out of sorts, or lost. Disorientation normally has a negative connotation. A moment of disorientation, when welcomed, can be a bridge to great enlightenment. Disorientation happens every time you encounter information or an experience that your mind cannot make meaning of. Disorientation forces you to evaluate what you see, hear, feel, and know. It is very important to welcome disorientation and develop awareness around it so that when it happens you respond by reflecting, rather than avoiding these feelings. (Perspective, p. 31)

TRIGGERS

In order to achieve mindwholeness, you have got to be aware of your triggers. Triggers can be associated with anything that reminds you of a traumatic memory. Jhené Aiko released a brilliant song called Triggered. In the song, she describes the difficulty of trying to navigate life in the midst of recovering from the devastating end of a relationship. The song recounts the many ways she is reminded of her trauma and the harsh reality of working through moving on. Knowing your triggers is so key to obtaining mindwholeness. Triggers can be any sound, smell, sight or anything else that initiates a tap dance on a painful memory in your mind. Again, being aware of what your triggers are can help you to respond appropriately, when they rise to the surface.

HOW YOU COPE

What coping behaviors do you employ to reduce or avoid a stressful situation? Knowing how you cope is necessary for mindwholeness. When you are aware of your coping patterns, you can more quickly assess any problems or situations to find the root of the problem and rectify the issue. That only happens when you are mindwhole.

STRESS RESPONSES AND RETENTION IN THE BODY

Your brain does not send you a text when it senses something is off in your environment. Unlike the heart, it can't beat faster or cramp up. So the brain sends silent alarms to the body to alert you to the fact that there is some trouble in your midst. If your brain is overwhelmed, then stress usually shows up in your body to alert you to stop what you are doing or to caution you to slow down. The connection between the brain and the body is an amazing thing. When you can feel stress in your body, this level of intrapersonal connection between the mind and the body is called proprioceptive awareness. We all respond to stress differently. For example, I typically carry stress in my shoulders, my neck, and my lower back. If you have ever had a good massage therapist, they are able to tell you specifically where your stress zones are and how to avoid carrying stress in your body. The stress that you feel in your body is a direct reaction to what your brain is processing. Pay attention to your body alarms.

We have to do what we can to protect the brain and remain mindwhole.

Knowledge and Learning

What is knowledge? Is there a such thing as universal truth?

This is such a tough chapter to write because if it wasn't for what I was taught, I wouldn't be who I am today. I acknowledge that. Storytelling and the passing down of social norms is what has preserved and protected culture for many generations. Information sharing is such an important part of the human experience and human development.

As an up and coming adult, growing in wisdom and grace daily, I recently came to be aware of the fact that knowledge is not static. Realizing this and reflecting on my life, there were so many times when additional information or knowledge could have been beneficial to me. I could have made wiser decisions. I could have avoided some heartache. I am so grateful that my lack of knowledge/information, did not kill me or delay my purpose.

Knowledge is static for some people because their knowledge has not been tested by a diversity of experiences or because they refuse to learn more. Yes, people can get to a point in life where they refuse to learn. Some people are so trapped in their patterns that following a course of action any different from what they know can be so alarming that they follow fear back into their comfort zone. People in this category are in a terrible place because knowledge is not fixed or absolute. What you know today will be invariably different from what you may know even after reading this chapter (big ups and shameless plug for the teaching author).

Fear of the unknown initiates fight or flight in the same way that being in a horrifying situation might. When you don't know or can't comprehend something, you become immediately defensive and resistant to whatever is around you. Your ability to receive new information is limited and your behavior can become erratic. Feeling like you have adequate knowledge and more importantly knowing how to apply that knowledge is a necessary security for the human construct.

We have to be open to learning consistently. Knowledge is not static; it evolves as we evolve. What I struggle with is the fact that I can only live from and pass on what I know. If I never know more, I will never attain more and never have more to share. Parents, teachers, role models and influencers have a responsibility to teach with a disclaimer: "This is what I know now. It presents as rock solid truth, but you may have a life experience that will present a different truth and that is ok. Go with what you know and grow as you go".

Knowledge translates as tacit or explicit knowledge. Tacit knowledge is rooted in experience and is based on what you know. For example, there is definitely skill required to teach someone how to swing a golf club. There is proper technique, but from student to student, execution of this knowledge will look slightly different. That is tacit knowledge - subjective to experience and somewhat difficult to pass onto others. Tacit knowledge is very much based on the teaching style and perspective of the individual/group in the position to initiate the delivery of knowledge. In most cases this can be a teacher, role model, or parent. Tacit knowledge is much harder to transfer for the purposes of learning. It is also important to point out that tacit knowledge very much contributes to an individual's perspective (Perspective, p. 31) and how they relate to the world.

On the other hand, explicit knowledge is rooted in data. Explicit knowledge is derived by what can be proven or what has been documented as scientific or historical fact. It is hard for a student to argue with explicit knowledge. In most cases, there is some methodology at work behind the scenes making this type of knowledge explicit. This methodology helps someone who is newly exposed to the information, prove and then repeatedly practice the method for application. To a certain degree, explicit knowledge can be easier to pass along and duplicate exactly from one person to another.

No matter how fixed we believe knowledge is it can evolve. As there are new developments, teachers have a responsibility to ensure that we share new developments and teach people to welcome new information. As a teacher, teaching other teachers, I have always shared two models that help us to understand our role as teachers and translators of information: **The Teacher-Student Duality Model** and the **Thomas Model of Individual Learning**. I am sharing these models in the bonus section of this book so that you can see your responsibility as a teacher to be continuously learning. These models will also help you to discern whether or not your students are excelling to the highest level of learning (teaching) or if they are merely a pass through for the information you are providing on a regular basis.

Learning happens everywhere. Bless my child for being my crash-test dummy for learning. She learns everywhere she goes! Everything in life is a lesson - from learning how to tie your shoes, to learning how to do advanced math, to learning how to read someone's energy. It is not enough for us to reduce learning to the classroom or to a period of developmental years in our lives. We must commit to being life-long learners – in pursuit of knowledge and learning in all experiences and as much as we possibly can.

Perspective

I am fascinated by the human experience. I am so fulfilled when I have the opportunity to sit with others and just listen to their story. I think there is something so useful in learning from others and their experiences (hence the impetus behind *Life Light*). In fact, I learn a great deal from my 1-1 interactions with others. I listen for meaning and I immediately apply anything useful that can benefit me or others. For almost an entire year, I focused on perspective as a teaching model. What was really profound to me was applying the definition of perspective to different individual's stories that I have observed over time to seek out deeper meaning in their stories.

Perspective is your point of view, your attitude, or your way regarding something. This is such a simple definition that has such a significant meaning. What I came to understand is that your perspective really drives how you interact with the world, people in the world, and the circumstances that you encounter every day in the world. Bias (judgement made from information gathered in perspective), opinion (articulation of perspective), and even what some people believe to be fact is all magnified by perspective.

One of my strengths as a person, counselor, professional, and advocate is my desire to really understand the perspective of the people I engage with on a regular basis. I want to understand what makes a person think the way they think and behave the way they behave.

I envision perspective as a verb: subconscious action happening in real time. Perspective applies itself as a layer, a lens if you will, when past experiences collide with a present reality. There is an outward action associated with the mental patterns that are happening in the background to drive behaviors triggered by perspective.

Envision a child that may have been bitten by a dog. The memory formed from that experience may be so tragic that it programs the child's mind to be fearful of dogs going forward. The next time a child interacts with a dog their perspective is what either prompts the child to hide behind their parents or to run ahead and fully engage with the dog. So I will say it again, **perspective happens when your past experiences collide with your present reality.** Perspective could be the light at the end of the tunnel that drives you to keep moving forward or it could be the cloud that darkens the path and prevents you from moving forward.

Pause here for a moment of reflection. Can you trace back any of your behaviors to a layer of perspective that you once had, that you later found out was not completely accurate? In other words, your perspective was wrong.

Through reflection and introspection, you can trace your perspective back to something you either experienced or were taught. If you are having a difficult time navigating something - a new relationship, a new job, a personal crisis, etc. it might be time to check your perspectives to see where there might be a blockage that will not allow you to move forward or ascend higher. Regular checks to your perspective are necessary. Stepping back to evaluate situations before making decisions or reacting is critical (when there is time in the decision making process to do so, of course). Perspective significantly impacts your future direction and the trajectory of your life.

See yourself as the captain of a ship named "Your Life". As the captain, you have a responsibility to ensure that you and everyone else on your ship arrives to their destination safely. As a captain, there are things that you will and will not have the ability to manage. In this example, I see perspective as having the wisdom to live in the balance between "steering the ship" (being in control) and "letting the chips fall where they may" (going with the flow). This is a weird juxtaposition I know, but hear me out. Pause and re-read this thought if you need to.

When you have clear perspective, you are able to sustain the level of effort required to keep the ship on course, by demonstrating an understanding of the reality that you cannot control any factors outside of steering the ship. Clear perspective allows you to release the potential anxiety that comes along with trying to steer + trying to steady the water + trying to keep the wind from blowing (like Storm from X-Men) + anything else that pulls you away from the task of steering. If water rises or the wind blows too hard, clear perspective allows you to keep focused on steering.

Clouded perspective on the other hand, would lead you to believe that you could in fact, steer the ship and manage all of the outside factors. Clouded perspective could also have you abandoning your post as captain and allowing the ship to sail into imminent crisis. There is a place of wisdom between those two approaches that is controlled by your perspective.

We want to aim for clear, evaluated, tried and true perspective. Keep your eyes on reaching your destination. If the wind blows, dig your feet in and prepare to fortify your position. If anything else that pops up unexpectedly, acknowledge it, do what you can, but put these things in their proper place of perspective and treat them accordingly.

ADAPTING PERSPECTIVE

Adapting perspective reminds me of real life air bending. Adapting an ingrained perspective, can be tough, like shifting an element as complex as the air. Have you ever seen the videos of the babies that put on glasses and see with 20/20 vision for the first time? Can you hear their joy, envision the smiles on their faces, appreciate the tears, or imagine their happy dance? I can see this so vividly. At the precise moment, when the lens is perfectly in front of their eyes, they are confronted by a different reality. For however many years they may be old, they could only interpret and understand information received from a limited perspective. Having a supportive device (the glasses) adapted their perspective. Friends, the perspectives that you have been living with for many years have to be adapted the same way. Sometimes the lens is a conversation with a friend or family member that helps you to see something differently. Other times it can be an experience that you live through, that helps you to see differently. Regardless, perspective has to be adapted for your own personal survival.

POWER OF OBJECTIVITY

Having clear perspective also helps you to walk in the power of objectivity. Let's pause here and talk about those four words: The Power of Objectivity. Remaining objective allows you to weed through emotional rhetoric and listen for meaning in the information that might be coming your way. As a literal thinker, I usually try to skip past all of the fat and get straight to the meat. Maintaining a level of objectivity is super important in how you receive, perceive, and then act on information. Clear perspective and objectivity can work together to help you make sound judgements and stay above the fray.

Let me be clear here though, objectivity is different than optimism. Optimism is putting a positive and hopeful spin on everything. I am sorry to break this news to you. Everything is not positive. Every situation is not hopeful. I am not advocating for you to be bright and sunny about everything that comes your way, I am advocating for you to be realistic, honest, and rational. So while optimism is a great way to approach life, remaining objective is a more useful approach. Clear perspective and objectivity help you see straight to the point.

LEARN TO APPRECIATE DISORIENTATION

Disorientation creates space for evaluation and helps you to develop mental agility. Awareness of your perspective also helps you to evaluate what you know versus what you see. This is not necessarily a principle of faith, but more aligned with objectivity. It is necessary that you reconcile reality with your perspective (Mindwholeness, p. 21).

Being aware of perspective and its power to control our view on life is crucial. I can say now that I am much more cautious and discreet in my approach to everything because I want to make sure my perspective is not skewed before I engage or proceed. I think having this understanding of how perspective works in the background certainly helps me to be more aware of myself and others. This level of awareness, discretion, and caution is an absolutely necessary skill if you are going to stay in the light and pursue your best self.

Trauma

More and more people are talking transparently these days - sharing experiences they have suffered through and eventually overcome. Whether it is social media influencers using their platform to empower people or watching the popularity of the #Metoo movement explode, "sharing is caring" is definitely the trend in this era of time. Things that for many years have been socially unacceptable to talk about are becoming more and more commonplace. This is great! Those of us "growing up" in this dispensation of time have the privilege of living out loud in a way that many of our predecessors did not. We have the ability to get free and be freed from baggage that has historically driven those who raised us to depression and in some cases suicide. But we can be free! You can be free today (Freedom, p. 83).

I was teaching a class on perspective and to frame my lesson, I used an example from a feature story that I read in a magazine about a single mother's great come back. According to the article, the woman had fallen on hard times and had lost everything in the process. She was begging for money as a means of income to care for herself and her child. After many days of not having enough to feed herself and her son, the woman met a wealthy man. The man felt compassion for her, saw beyond her temporary state of desperation and committed to providing her with the financial resources she needed to get back on her feet. (Let me pause right here and say don't get stuck in your present circumstances. A shift will come and things will get better.) This man's random act of kindness propelled her into her next place of purpose. As far as readers know, this woman and her son lived happily ever after. This was such an amazing story of harmony in the human experience. Don't we all love happy endings?

Prior to preparing to teach this lesson on perspective, trauma was a concept that I did not think I had much experience with, on a practical level. I had always associated trauma with some horrific tragedy that leaves people dead or broken beyond repair. From my hospital drama TV show watching days, I was familiar with Dr. Hunt who is a trauma doctor. His specialty is treating people that have been stabbed, or have lost an arm in an accident, or have fallen out of a building and developed a life-threatening head injury. To me these instances screamed trauma - someone needed immediate, expert intervention and medical attention because they were clinging onto life, as a result of some unfortunate event.

Take a moment to compare the examples of trauma from the TV show to my teaching illustration of the single mother in need. In my teaching example, no one died tragically and the main character of the story was not bleeding uncontrollably. However, the single mom lived through an extremely stressful and overwhelming situation. The single mother and her son endured through their very own traumatic situation.

Single parents take so many life hits that they do not talk to anyone about. Having to stand by and watch all of your possessions be repossessed is distressing enough for an individual alone, but these hits can be especially distressing for a single parent. Then, scanning the periphery of the scene and realizing that your child is in your shadow watching this happen, is even more devastating.

Having to process all of this turbulence can be so overwhelming that a person can go into cardiac arrest. Not feeling like you have a grip on your circumstances and the matters of your livelihood can have the same wounding effect psychologically, as taking a bullet to the heart. When I stepped back from the article and really reflected on this woman's story, I realized that she had indeed suffered from trauma and more importantly that she was living her days with some post-traumatic stress. I dug a little deeper into her story and learned that this woman had experienced trauma (possibly multiple traumas) in her life, which significantly impacted her perspective and also her behavior. For the first time, my understanding of the significant impact and devastation that trauma can cause was truly awakened.

Many of us have suffered trauma (big or small) and we just keep on living. Kudos to you for surviving! How much healthier would we be as a people, if we were encouraged to be aware of and work through the trauma we have experienced over the years? Who is shining the light on the people who suffer trauma and are trying so hard to keep pushing forward every day? We are - right here, right now! Let's get into it.

For my own personal edification, I explored the definition of trauma (because I love words). I did not like Webster's definition and I did not like what dictionary.com offered, so for the sake of teaching, I came up with my own.

Trauma is the imprint left on a person (physical, emotional, psychological, or spiritual) as a result of an intensely stressful experience, moment, or circumstance.

Trauma shows up in so many different ways that the totality of the concept cannot be captured easily. There is no one-way to treat "trauma". The result of trauma or the aftershocks can be addressed through a variety of healing, wholeness, and self-care methods. Having an understanding of what trauma is, can determine how you handle yourself and others.

I have always been the type of person to just keep pushing. No matter what happens, just keep pushing. Feelings get hurt, just keep pushing. Disappointment happens, just keep pushing. No after no, just keep pushing. If you cannot tell by now, my modus operandi is to just keep pushing. Not focusing on my own personal trauma was in some ways a coping mechanism that helped me to see past the trauma, but prevented me from actually dealing with the effects of trauma in my personal life.

I never once thought that my intensely stressful experiences qualified as trauma because in my story, there were no bullet holes or stab wounds, no ambulance sirens, and more importantly there was no Dr. Hunt running in to address my needs as a trauma patient. The intense stress - that was real! The feelings of hopelessness - so real! Stress eating and soothing - BIG real. The inability to occasionally focus and make decisions - so real. Anxiety that tried to take my very breath - mad real. The bouts of depression - totally real! The isolation - also real. How could trauma happen to me and I did not realize it? So now, with this new understanding of trauma, I spent some time in self-reflection to dig deeper into my own story and to scan my life for traumatic moments that I had potentially glossed right over in an effort to just keep pushing.

Here's how trauma happened to me and I didn't even know – so I recently lost a little weight and have developed a new habit for lingering in the bathroom mirror longer than I probably should, on any given day. But what can I say, she bad!!! During one of my mirror dates, I noticed a scar. Now I knew the scar was there, but I had never given it much attention. Now, without the weight, the scar is visible all of the time. Not only can I see the scar, but other people could possibly see the scar. They may have questions about this scar that I am not prepared to discuss. It had been hidden for so long and even though I knew in the back of my mind the scar was there, I refused to give it any power or meaning in my life.

All of a sudden, all of these years later, I could see the damage that had been done to my body. I remembered the pain associated with the scar. I could feel the tenderness around the scar - there to continuously remind me that it was there and still very much alive. I see the scar regularly, when I am supposed to be getting my mind ready to conquer the day. The scar is unavoidable. I realized I had done what many of us do when we endure a traumatic experience - we ignore it. We build walls around it or we bury it in hopes that it never sees the light of day again. We do everything in our power (sometimes sub-consciously) to avoid having to deal with our trauma. We try to numb our feelings and suppress memories, to keep from having to feel what we felt in that moment ever again. These are all fair reactions. However, there comes a time when we have to deal with where and when we have been wounded.

Now with the reality of the scar bombarding me every morning, my mirror visits are different - I am disoriented. I have two options: ignore the scar by trying to alter my behavior in some ridiculous way that will hide the scar from plain sight or deal with the scar. I decided to deal with the scar.

For the first time in over a decade, I had to pay attention to the color of the scar. I had to pay attention to the location of the scar. And now that I could see it every time I passed by the mirror, I had no choice but to address the lingering feelings I was unaware that I had about the scar. Looking back many years, I started by acknowledging to myself that I was actually wounded - flesh sliced opened, internal organs exposed, blood everywhere. Memories flooded my mind - voices, faces, feelings, and sounds. All of these memories reminded me of the moment my trauma happened. I realized that in the moment, I had been completely helpless and could not control what was happening to me. I remember feeling like less than a person. In a real, legitimate way my life had been in jeopardy. I could have died.

All of a sudden all of these emotions that I didn't even realize were tied to this scar came to the surface. I kept replaying the memories from years ago - watching a past version of myself suffer and trying to understand why I did not pay attention to the fact that trauma was happening to me.

That is what trauma does - it can cause us to shut down and close off in a way that makes us unable to recalibrate or regain footing in a particular situation. After watching the playback of my story in my mind several times, I realized that in that moment, many years ago, living was my priority! It did not matter what was happening to me. I could take it - as long as I lived through it. I did not have a strategy for living through my trauma. In fact, many of the details are a blur to me now. I was in a game of the survival of the fittest and my will to see my daughter live a full life kept me fighting for my life.
I kept pushing.

Trauma has the ability to change the nature of who we are as individuals and it can dictate how we interact with the people in our space. Trauma causes a tear in the fabric of your life and if it is left unaddressed, the fabric will continue to tear until it is no longer useful. I am not encouraging you to run head first into traumatic experiences that you may have had throughout the course of your life. I do think however, that it is important for you to acknowledge what trauma is and when/where it may have occurred in your life. It is very possible that your traumatic experiences may not be extreme enough to require a sexy trauma surgeon, but there are still interdependent parts of you that need to be made whole. An approach to remedy trauma includes acknowledging the trauma, addressing the trauma, healing from the trauma, and then reflecting briefly on the trauma (AAHR). For the sake of making a thing, a thing, let's call this the **AAHR** (pronounced air) **Method for Navigating Trauma:**

ACKNOWLEDGE

I have been very fortunate but also very intentional about surrounding myself with people who want the best for me and push me to my next and greatest level in potential. In moments of transition, it is always important to have someone to keep you accountable and to help you unpack your experiences. I had the privilege of interacting with a very kind soul who asked questions that were very uncomfortable for me to answer. It wasn't so much the questions that were uncomfortable, it was my having to share from a wounded place that made the questions uncomfortable. Through my wanting to be vulnerable with this person, I was able to actually talk about feelings and emotions that I had not acknowledged for many years. Vulnerability allows you to feel, to heal, and to move forward. When you do not have space to be vulnerable, accountable, and psychologically safe it can be difficult for you to transcend where you are today.

Acknowledging trauma does not make you less of a person. Having to speak something painful out loud to yourself or to others can be terrifying. Fear can be paralyzing with this step of healing from trauma. Maybe you are afraid that someone will know what happened to you. Acknowledging when there has been a traumatic experience in your life is almost very similar to giving forgiveness. Acknowledging trauma may free you up in a way that: clears your head, clears your heart, clears your soul, and cleanses your physical body of the traumatic experience. But don't be afraid to start there - what happened, happened. What is done, is done. Now that you have completed this step, you can move on.

ADDRESS
There are so many ways to address traumatic experiences in your life. It's important for you to know what you can handle and what will actually bring about healing for you!!! Many people journal. Journaling is a great way to reflect, to see the progression in your thoughts, and it is a great way to "talk" about something without actually verbalizing it.

Go to therapy! There are so many technological innovations that have made therapy available on demand and easy to access. Whether you pursue individual therapy, couple's therapy, group therapy, or family therapy, find a safe space for you to talk out loud about your feelings and to be challenged by others who are skilled to help you navigate the trauma.

Work through the trauma artistically. Write a song. Design a mural. Grab an old school set of watercolors, a cup of water, and paint it out. Pick a song that moves you and dance.

These are just a few examples of the many different ways to get at the problem. The important thing is that you actually take action. We can only pursue powered living when we are actually directing the actions to move us forward. It might require that you have to address the person or people that caused the trauma. In many cases you have to determine whether or not this is something that will help you heal or something that will hurt you more. And if it's something that will hurt you more, then you have to find a way to heal without actually addressing the person or situation directly.

HEAL

I separated healing from acknowledging and addressing traumatic experiences. Healing requires consistent, deliberate energy be directed towards the action of healing. Healing is not something that you can just call out into the atmosphere and boom...it shows up. There is a movement behind healing that has to happen and that requires you creating new boundaries, new behaviors, new thought paths, and new perspectives that helps you to keep putting one foot in front of the other. Healing takes time. Healing is also not a one-time deal. Healing is a commandment that you have to start living by. In the same way that you might practice other affirmations, you have to affirm your healing. Whether your trauma was physical, emotional, psychological, or spiritual there is a healing process available to get you back to wholeness.

REFLECT BRIEFLY

We should always be in a place of reflection. I mean, I think we are always in our head. We think about everything, but reflection is spending time focusing on something intentionally. Let me be clear here - there is a place of balance between reflection and overthinking. I have some friends who are super deep thinkers and they get so deep in their thoughts that they can't even move forward. It is like they get paralyzed by their thought process. I am not encouraging you to open up or revisit experiences that have been traumatic for you in a way that causes paralysis. However, I am suggesting that reflection helps you to see your power, your resilience, and your strength as a person to move forward in liberty.

We are constantly evolving and that evolutionary process requires that we're in a constant state of self-awareness and self-analysis. Reflecting briefly can help you to realize how much you've changed (good, bad, or indifferent) since the traumatic experience. Reflecting briefly can help you to self-assess and determine if there is a "type of person" that might be harmful to you. Reflecting briefly allows you to see yourself transparently and it also helps you to see what else you need to do to cope, heal, and get better. Finally, reflecting briefly helps you to continue to see where there is work that needs to be done. Don't shy away from that truth. You cannot blossom if you are not pruned from time to time.

This is your life. Do what you need to do to heal - your way and in your perfect time.

PS. I wish I could reach out and hold every reader's hand to reassure you that you are strong and that you can get through this. There are many qualified counselors and mental health professionals that can listen to you and help you develop a strategy for making peace with your trauma.

Mental Health Resources (Please reach out if you need some help!):

- Call 911 if you require immediate attention

- www.mentalhealth.gov or call 1-877-726-4727

- http://finder.psychiatry.org/

- https://www.zocdoc.com/

BOOK 1

Reflections

Your Role in Vision

It is important to know your role in bringing vision to life. Visionaries see the end result. Most visionaries are extremely passionate and enthusiastic. This is a level of energy that every idea and every project needs to get mobilized. Visionaries see something magical that moves people to action. Many times though, visionaries are unable to carry out their vision alone, because their role is to see - not necessarily to do.

There are other contributors to vision who are incredible at hearing the vision and bringing it to fruition. Let's call these folks the executors (not executioners!!!). Executors are designed to get it done, by any means necessary. Executors are gifted to hear and see at the same time — which is an ability that is often overlooked. Executors have the tough task of carrying the weight of vision to completion and they often receive none of the glory for a job well done.

It is so important that you know if you are a visionary or an executor. That way, you do not waste energy trying to walk a path not designed for you. Additionally, it is important for you to know which one you are, so that you can surround yourself with the right types of people. If you are a visionary, you need a circle of executors. Otherwise, you and your visionary friends will be stuck with a multiplicity of ideas that you cannot bring to fruition. Similarly, if you are an executor, you need to be sure there are visionaries in your circle that can help you see when you're stuck in the details. We have to learn how to work in tandem to get ish done.

Stay In The Now

The present (what is happening now - in this moment) should get the majority of your attention. The past cannot be changed and the future cannot be controlled.

Only look back to the past, as an archeologist or an analyst for clues to inform your present and future, but leave the fossils behind. Leave the future to the greatest power and you will get to where you are supposed to be at the appointed time. Trust this truth and stay present.

Manifest

What you manifest is literally what shows up - everywhere you are. Sometimes you have to manifest an alternate (positive) reality, until you reach that place. That is why regular self-affirmation is so important. Sometimes you have to speak peace into chaos until you reach your place of peace. Or you may have to speak prosperity into a moment of limited resources. You are what you manifest. Manifest greatness!

On Words...

Words are so extremely powerful. They are the vehicles that we use to move thoughts and feelings. I am a 100% geek and I have an affinity for words. Don't judge me – my truth.

The power behind your words can break a person down or bring about their healing - literal life or death. All the words matter. That should be a hashtag...#allwordsmatter! The words you choose to wear on something as simple as a t-shirt sends a message to others or the message associates you with a group/organization before you even say anything. The words you plaster on the back of your car bumper sends a message to drivers behind you. The words you choose to hang up on posters and pictures on the walls of your home or office communicate messages to you - over and over again.

Pay attention to the words you use. Are you creating environments for you (and others) to thrive? Or are you being defeated by the messages you are taking in regularly? I choose to live and have chosen to use my words to help other people pursue powered living.

Say more with less!

BOOK 2
Being

Connectedness

As I get older, I am becoming increasingly more aware of how important it is to be connected to others. In the grand scheme of things, life is a small fragment of time.

What matters most?

How much you know and how much you have earned?

Or is it more significant to be mindful of how many lives you have touched and how many lives have touched yours? I believe it is the latter. We thrive through connection to others. We learn kindness as a child from the cashier at the grocery store that knows your name (at least I did growing up...before self-checkout became a thing). We learn how to handle varying degrees of responsibility, from the teachers that use their influence positively, at different stages of our life to shape us into responsible human beings. Also, we learn how to love through nurturing and disappointing interactions with others. Many of the lessons we learn and many of the successes we have in life can be directly attributed to the connections we have to other people.

So that you understand my intention in this chapter, I want you to pay attention to the fact that I am using the term connectedness instead of relationship. I want your brain to process what I am saying differently. I want you to think deeper and more broadly about the concepts in this chapter. Got it? Think about this - when I say relationship, who is the first person you thought of?

Did you think of a current, past, or future significant other? If I am correct, that is because the idea that your relationship with a spouse/significant other is consistently reinforced as the highest level of relationship that we as a people can aspire to. I can't say that I agree with that idea. I have friends of all backgrounds that (to some degree) measure their success as a person by their marital status. I also know others that have married out of desperation and their relationships end on terrible terms. Whether this reinforcement of the idea of a primary relationship is intentional or not, it is happening, at somewhat alarming rates (alarming to me at least).

If you think about this honestly and without bias for one moment, you may realize that you actually have stronger (connections) with your family or friends than you do with your significant other. You may even try to convince yourself that your highest relationship is with your significant other, when really, it is not. If reading this felt a little uncomfortable, take a deep breath and keep reading. Your brain is just trying to process through the disorientation. Remember what I said before, disorientation is helpful. It opens your eyes to the possibility that new information coming in could be different, but true.

It is ok to have a deeper connection with someone than you do with your spouse. It doesn't mean that you love your spouse any less, it just means that you are capable of giving and receiving deeper love through your connection with someone else. And just so that I do not get protestors at future book events, I am not suggesting that you love someone deeper, in a way that leads to infidelity. It is possible for you to love your parent, child, or best friend more than your significant other. Yes - it totally is possible. I am a huge proponent for marriage and for significant others cleaving or clinging to each other (this is a whole other lesson for another book). But let's not allow the world to manipulate our thinking to see the spousal connection as the highest connection. The depth of your love for someone, as compared to another, really does not matter. It is how you cultivate all of your connections that really matters. Read this again. (Cultivating, p. 116)

So back to what I was saying initially about connectedness (before I had to teach that little lesson). What I am learning is that connectedness is really the deepest measure of a successful life. Your connection to yourself and to others is everything. Connectedness is next level mindfulness. I say this because connectedness also focuses on your awareness of others - individually and in groups. Connectedness requires a level of reciprocity and intentionality that is not required in relationship. Check the definitions of the two words for yourself. There are some connections that can never be undone regardless of space, time, or circumstances. That's how deep connectedness is - almost like trying to unweave a spider's web. You get it now? Connectedness - that is what we are talking about.

As I reflected on connectedness, I thought about the fact that I have always had a very independent spirit. So much so, that when I was younger, I thought I could do everything on my own. I severed connections with people in a heartbeat. No sweat off my back - total savage. I limited my networks to people and groups that I believed benefitted me most (at that moment). I didn't think about the long term consequences of my behaviors or what I may need down the road. What is really bizarre to me, is that I have genuinely cared for people, their development, and their wellbeing all of my life. How could I think that neglecting my connections was a healthy behavior that would somehow benefit me in the long run?

I believed in myself and thought that as long as I had me, I was good. Wrong. I fumbled and stumbled along for quite some time until I realized, I was mostly alone trying to navigate life. There are definitely benefits to being alone from time to time, but creating situations of complete isolation is detrimental to your wellness. You should be finding ways to grow and thrive in every evolution of your life. Having people around to agitate you enough to grow and sprinkle enough goodness on you to help you thrive makes all of the difference. I realize now, that I missed the mark for so long on this one. Thank goodness for grace, patience, forgiveness, and restoration.

So my savage years came to a screeching halt and I had to come to terms with the fact that I had not nurtured connections over the years. I didn't check on people when they were on my mind. I missed birthdays, weddings, children being born all because no one told me how important it is to hold onto the people that you love. Well, maybe I knew this deep down inside. It just didn't register to me how important this was. As the years went by, the death of loved ones drew closer to me. The perfect world that we lived in went to crap.

Mass murders became an almost daily news headline. School shootings became commonplace. People of faith were murdered in their place of faith. Everyday hardworking people gunned down for no reason, just trying to earn enough money to feed their kids. The world (and maybe my naive perception of the world) ceased to exist. That is when the light came on for me. Life is only a moment – a brief period of time. Who you see today, you may not see tomorrow. The key to a full life is in your connections.

This is me talking to myself - go with me:

Me to Me: "you legit have no idea how many days you have left on this earth... you need to change the way you love the people in your life."

Slam...just like that...a pile of bricks on my head, a dagger to my heart, and me rolling around on the floor in the most dramatic way possible.

Me to me, again: "Yo, you have really been a jerk to people. Let's ask for forgiveness, rebuild broken connections, be present for others, and never do that again. Ok?

Me to Me: Yes me, I got it!"

Connectedness matters my friends, it matters.

I struggled with connectedness for many years. I didn't know that I was an introvert and subsequently didn't understand how I was designed to give and receive energy. Having this level of awareness of myself, now, is so meaningful to me. That said, I cannot completely blame my reckless behavior solely on the character trait of introversion and my innate desire to want to stay to myself. I acknowledge that some of my decisions to cut people off were rooted in pride and were hotheaded. You hurt me – I do not need you. That approach (in some cases) was immature.

There were other times that I isolated myself; to invest my energy in other places that I eventually learned would be a shortsighted and temporary investment. Despite failed attempts to reframe my thinking then, I can see now how this was a mistake. We are connected to one another in so many different ways. In fact, what I appreciate about the modern day concept of diversity is that it teaches us to value difference in the same way that we have valued commonality for so long. Think about that and possibly rethink your openness to diversity in every aspect of your life. Even in difference, there is still value in being connected and having to navigate reconciling that difference together. Connectedness is required - if we are to have full and whole lives.

NECESSITY FOR CONNECTION TO OTHERS

Science suggests that connection is a requirement for healthy and whole lives. Whether it is being on the giving or receiving end of affirmation, a gentle caress on your face or wanting the attention of someone else, the human experience requires a level of connectedness. Think about the one or two (or more) people that you must talk to each day in order to feel a sense of contentment. Even though I am a fully grown person, I speak to both of my parents during my afternoon commute every day. There is something very soothing about being able to release negative vibes from my day to the people that care for me most, but more importantly, having the opportunity to hear what is new in their day is the nourishment (and laughter lots of times) that I need to keep going. This is a connection that is mutually beneficial and has significant importance to me. Why? Because connections matter!

In 2019, we live in a very complicated world. The innocence of life is being snatched away. As a society, we are not always as concerned and caring for one another as we should be. I have realized the greater value in connection as I have watched the people that I love most get older and wiser, but slower. I have lived through losing loved ones that were near and dear to my heart. Watching these life transitions has significantly influenced the value that I place on connection. Now, I better understand the need for intentionality in connectedness. I am more inclined to check in to confirm that the ones I love are content. In many ways, knowing that my loved ones are content, gives me a sense of inner peace.

Connection is not always long term or eternal. There are some people that you can connect with for a short time or even in passing and still feel the influence of their presence in your life as if you have known them intimately for many years. Knowing this, I have developed a greater intensity for making every moment count. Rather than passing a moment off as insignificant or assuming that a moment will repeat itself, I have learned to be more flexible and patient with others. I have learned a level of self-sacrifice that is required to reciprocate in connectedness. I have learned to observe and to listen to others. I listen to listen - not to compare similar life stories, but to be present with them. For some people, your presence or your listening ear may be the best gift you could ever give. Be intentional about connecting.

RESPONSIBILITY IN CONNECTION

No matter how long a connection with someone lasts, there is a responsibility on everyone's part to be honest and to maintain relational integrity. Connections are not one sided - we both have to work. More than doing the work, we need to be on the same page for the purpose of the connection - is this an acquaintanceship, a friendship, or are we in deep connection (familial or romantic). Being aligned in this space makes it so much easier for two people to walk together and work together. No excuses - be a responsible human.

EVOLUTION OF CONNECTION

As we evolve as individuals, it is necessary that our connections evolve as well. I think we struggle here a lot. At least, I did. No one ever really explained the beauty and pain in growing up and growing old together. I am not the same person that I was at 17 years old or even 23 years old. That said, there has to be space given for me to continue to adapt and evolve. I have to give myself space (and grace – Grace, p. 97), by listening to my heart, my mind, and more importantly, my soul. Your personal compass has a way of telling you exactly what you need to know at exactly the right time. Listen and be willing to walk in your truth. Communicate to others that things are changing for you - even if you do not know how things are changing. The importance of communication (even in uncertainty) cannot be stressed enough.

Similarly, we have to follow the same path in our connections to others. I was not taught this concept and its relevance in marriage. If you take the traditional vows in marriage and don't customize them for your situation or your generation, you are likely taking unrealistic vows. "From this day forward", is such a huge commitment for two people to make without knowing how to evolve together and appreciating the value of evolving together in connectedness. This is especially true, if people are not committed to challenging each other to evolve; and then respecting and supporting the evolution. When two people can commit to seeing each other through change versus trying to keep each other bound to being the same person you were when you met, connections can thrive. This healthy, equitable love is what we call connectedness, ladies and gentlemen.

SEVERING CONNECTION

In the same vain, it is very important that when you reach a point of needing to sever a connection with someone that you do so responsibly. There are many reasons why connections should be severed. If connections are not psychologically, emotionally, or physically safe, go your separate ways. Being the bigger person is a real life vibe that does not always pay anything in return. Sometimes you have to see a greater need and be willing to make a sacrifice, to ensure your wellbeing and the wellbeing of others that may suffer as collateral damage in your situation. Ask for help - potentially outside of your normal circles. Having a neutral third party to hear you and help you find your way through your feelings and ideas is so helpful.

CONNECTEDNESS AND PURPOSE

We reach purpose through connectedness. We are created to be stewards (Stewardship, p. 112) to one another. By definition, a steward acts as a surrogate for someone else – metaphorically responsible for helping to carry certain elements of someone's purpose. We have the responsibility to demonstrate care for others. Without connectedness on some level, there is no avenue through which you can attain your greatest purpose (Purpose, p. 103).

In all that I have said in this chapter (and I recognize that I have said A LOT), I hope that you have a deeper understanding of the importance of nurturing your connections. It is very possible that you have been hip to the game much longer than I have. If that is the case, kudos to you. Continue to spread your goodness to the world through the connections that you make. Tell people that you love them. Show people that you care. Maximize every moment that you have left to grace the world's stage with your presence.

Love

Love as a concept is really incomprehensible. Think about it. How can you measure how much someone loves you? You can't. Love is so deep and so diverse. Love has no specific form or shape. Love doesn't look the same or feel the same for everyone. One of the greatest lessons in life is learning how to love and how to be loved unconditionally.

Love is very much a learned behavior - the same as learning how to tie your shoes. How you are loved or how you experience love significantly impacts the way that you understand and reciprocate love. Love is so broad. There is no way that I could even scratch the surface on the fullness of love with one chapter from a book. I can share what I have learned about love, in hopes that it helps you to identify and appreciate love in your life.

(Sidenote before we get started - I recognize that the etymology for the English word "love" takes root in many different versions of the word in other languages. For the sake of discussion, I am using the English word "love" to apply to various types of connections.)

There are behaviors that consistently reinforce the way a person feels towards you - the way they care for you. There is not one singular thing that someone can do or say that can truly represent the depth of what love looks like for that person. If someone says they love you, take that to the bank. Take it as far as it will go.

Love cannot and should not be classified, questioned, or tried. When we begin to question love, what we are actually doing is questioning: someone's commitment, their trustworthiness, and/or their ability to prioritize you. Be clear on that. Just because you may feel indifference from someone does not mean that they do not love you.

If it stops feeling like love to you, don't be afraid to follow another path. Love that becomes toxic can be deadly. I observed a lot of volatility in connections between spouses growing up. As a child, watching love on display, it didn't seem full of joy. Love didn't seem like a place of protection. Love didn't seem even truly possible and as a result, I grew up not trusting in relationships. Looking back, I realize that I probably jumped into adult matters that I wasn't quite prepared for because in some ways I didn't have enough positive reinforcement of what love is, to really understand how to interact with it properly.

It wasn't until I had a child, that I really recognized that I am still learning how to grasp and completely understand what love means. In many respects, I liken my role as a parent to the role of the creator. As a parent, you watch your child constantly navigating the various developmental stages in life. You are there when they run too hard into a wall and need to be reassured that everything will be ok. You guide them just enough for them to be independent, but to trust that you will have their back no matter what. You try to teach them as much as you can, before they are convinced that they know everything. You watch your child develop from a small seed to an intricate being, with complex thoughts, opinions, and perspectives. You sit back and marvel in all of these moments with pride and gratitude.

Being part of my child's evolution, opened my heart and my mind to really understand what love is and how it can be expressed. Experiencing this depth of love, what I believe is truly unconditional love, encourages me to share love without condition to others. Love should not be stifled by our limited experience with it. There is no right way to love. We just have to keep trying at it until we hit the love jackpot.

Love is diverse and multi-faceted. Real love is necessary. Love heals and makes us whole. Love binds us together as a people. Love insulates us from the hatred in this world. Love helps us to overcome and fight for who/what we believe in. Love helps us to see beyond mistakes, wrongdoings, issues, problems, and circumstances to develop truly divine connections with one another.

If you love someone, tell them. Our days are too short for you to overthink and not share your truth.

Children

We all have a responsibility to raise someone up to walk in our footsteps. Whether you are a parent, teacher, or mentor, you have an important space of influence in someone's life. I could teach a class for the rest of my life on all of the things that I have learned about myself, my child, and the world we live in – based on just the 10 years that she has blessed this earth with her presence. Even after preparing the syllabus for this class, I would still have enough teaching content to teach another lifetime.

Every day with a child, is a new lesson, a new journey. In many ways, raising children is another evolutionary circle that is not fixed upon anything concrete. Parents (I am speaking for all of us) spend a great deal of time feeling our way through the unknown - stepping on Legos along the way. There is no right way to parent, but I feel like this responsibility should come with a huge warning label. WARNING: YOU ARE RESPONSIBLE FOR DEVELOPING AN IMPRESSIONABLE LITTLE HUMAN - DON'T BE A JERK (or else they will grow up to be jerks). I am smiling to myself about all of the times that this warning label, with various other warnings, would have been helpful.

At this point, my kid is 10, so I still haven't navigated the teen beat, college years, or young adult life. I am sure there are many of you reading this that have fully grown children or grandchildren. As veterans in the game, we need you to keep reading in solidarity with us. Although my kid only has a decade under her belt, I have survived enough poopy underpants, crying spells, and incredible moments of empowerment to know that I have earned the platinum mom badge.

Raising children (yours or someone else's), is quite possibly the most important human responsibility ever (besides continuously raising yourself). For this responsibility to carry so much weight, I feel like taking care of kids should have been a required course in college. Forget the complex subjects like chemistry or calculus, developing an understanding of the investment required to raise children is a missed academic marketplace. It is a beautiful thing! I just wish someone would have schooled me on what I should be prepared for - not in a literal way, but "best practices", if you will (that is so corporate of me to throw that in there - but it felt fitting).

First things first (rest in peace Uncle Phil) - children are EXPENSIVE (see what I did there - there's the warning label that I so desperately needed). I grew up taking care of everyone else's children. I was always babysitting or holding someone else's baby in church. The benefit of this practice was that on a fundamental level, I was prepared to at least make sure my kid was clean, clothed, and fed. All of the babies that I babysat always came with a full diaper bag, so I had no idea how much it cost to keep a baby clean, clothed and fed. Diapers and formula alone are enough to break anyone's wallet (because the richer you are the more expensive the formula and organic diapers are). No one told me how much it cost to keep growing kids in clothes, jackets, and shoes. Like you can literally buy your kid a whole new wardrobe for school in August and then by October - they fit nothing. NOTHING - you hear me. No one told me that.

Then, there is child care - because working parents have to pay someone to keep their kids while they are at work earning the money to pay said child care people. I understand that childcare is likely comparable to the cost of living in your regional area, but we put a kid through day care in the DC metropolitan area....so somebody say "BIG BUCKS". Like bucks so big, our child care costs could pay for a whole three-bedroom house in other parts of the country. So child care alone - totally a whole 12-week class, at a minimum.

Then comes making home owning decisions. A whole other thing that I could have used some schooling on. So apparently where you buy your home is where your kids go to school. And even though the houses may be really nice, the schools can be total trash (not that this has been my experience - eye roll - yeah right). Buying a home is a major investment, just like having children. It makes sense that your kid would go to school in the neighborhood that you live in, but that did not compute for me until it was time for me to actually send the kid to school. Needless to say, after making a major investment to own the home we wanted, we still had to pay for our kid to go to private school because the public schools in our district were trash.

Note to new and aspiring parents: You may already know all of this and if you do - God bless you! But I didn't and I could have made much better decisions, if I had. If you have old people in your life (that you trust), that want to share information with you - especially about kids - do yourself a favor and listen.

Raising kids is like McDonald's All Day Breakfast. In concept, it is a great idea. The reality, however, is very different from the way it is advertised. Theoretically speaking, breakfast is supposed to be available all day, 24/7. However, if you go to

McDonald's at an off-breakfast time, you will likely experience a team that is not prepared to actually serve you breakfast. The hash browns have to be cooked fresh, so you have to wait. It is also likely that you will be served a stale biscuit that has been sitting in the warmer since 10:30am (when breakfast ended). The same gamble you take ordering hot cakes at 4pm, is the same gamble you take raising children.

Parents are on-call all day, every day (even on a romantic getaway or kidcation). But it doesn't mean that you're always prepared or fresh for that matter. Sometimes kids experience stale parents - especially when we are trying to balance the weight of the world without our kids seeing how stressful that really is. Or if your body really needed an extra 45 minutes of sleep, but your kid decides that watching cartoons at 3:45am is more important - you definitely get stale Mom at 3:45am and for the rest of that day if we are totally honest.
(Stay In The Now, p. 49)

Similarly, having kids is like having a mirror dangle in front of you reflecting your behaviors (good, bad, or indifferent) all of the time. Kids see everything, hear everything, and feel everything. It is so important that you do the best with the information that you have in real time. You will absolutely make mistakes, but you also have the opportunity to make choices that cultivate healthy lifestyles for your children. Consistently invest in your children. You reap what you sow as soon as your children are able to walk and talk.

Last, but certainly not least, children are givers of unconditional love - don't taint that. (Love, p. 65). Unconditional love is a concept that I tried to create in many failed friendships and relationships before having a child. It just seemed like if I could focus all of my thoughts and energy towards seeing past someone's faults that I could earn my unconditional love merit badge. Doesn't work like that. I subjected myself to verbal, physical, and psychological abuse all in an attempt to try to emulate unconditional love. Fast forward many years and God blesses me with a little person - who SEES me all of the time, whether I see myself or not. Even at my very worst - she loves me. There is an interconnectedness that we have that is indescribable.

Beyond the way she sees me, I see her. I have literally known her all of her life. That's something that only parents can say about their kids - that makes me feel cool (sorry...big nerd alert). But when I think about her and her potential in this earth, I know that I would risk it all to make sure she makes it to wherever God has for her to go.

In somewhat of a catastrophic time for me recently (heavy on the drama - just go along with me), I paused for a moment at my daughter's bedside. I was overwhelmed with emotion from every angle.

1. How could God think I was worthy enough to parent this amazing human?

2. How is it possible to love my baby more than anyone or anything else in this world - myself included?

3. How do I help her to really understand and walk in her full potential as a human being?

The answer was so simple and complex at the same time – "just keep doing what you're doing".

This was my midnight reflection, at her bedside, as her breathing soothed me: I would try to swim the length of the ocean to meet her needs. I would battle the incessant heat of the desert to protect her peace. Silly me - I would even try walking on fire or swimming with sharks. I would go to the most extreme of extremes to guarantee her safety, preserve her innocence, and ensure that her life fulfills the purpose for which it was given. I am so grateful to be the guardian of her gifts. She is infinity to me.

Children are A LOT, but their worth in your life and in the world is immeasurable.

Peace to you.

BOOK 2
Reflections

Identity

Just like knowledge and many other concepts covered in this book, identity is evolutionary. Have you run into someone that you have not seen in a while and they have said to you, "Wow, you've changed"? Yes, you may have changed. That's ok - especially if the change was intentional.

We are not created to be one dimensional beings. There are so many layers to who we are as individuals. Get to know who you are - at home by yourself, 1-1 with someone, in a group setting, etc. It is important for you to be comfortable in your own skin. There are so many layers to our identity - traversing layers is ok - we were not created to be one-dimensional.

Reputation

I had an epiphany not long ago that you cannot control how and when people speak on your character. I guess I have never really cared much about people's opinion about me. Even in failure - I know that I am great (my daddy told me so). So I had never really given any thought about the conversations people have about me when I am not in the room, until someone slipped up and mentioned that they had "just been talking about me".

This made me reflect on the number of conversations that could possibly be happening about me that I am not and may never be aware of. That was an instant gut check. My gut said "Listen kid...make sure you live your life in a way that people only have positive things to say about you". It is your choice what mark you leave on this earth. Only leave people with great things to say about you. You never know when and where your name will come up.

Own Your Shit (O.Y.S.)

Every now and then, you have to "talk to the people the way they need to be talked to"! It is so important for you to own your shit. You will make mistakes, but be quick to admit your fault. Forgive yourself and forgive others. Ask for forgiveness - even if you cannot identify anything that you've done wrong. Forgiveness is an act of purification that humbles you in the process. Walk in the weight of the responsibility of your truth. (SAY THAT OUT LOUD ONE TIME FOR THE PEOPLE IN THE BACK).

Walk in the weight (pause)

Of the responsibility (pause)

Of your truth (pause)

Do not create space for regret. Man up and live your best life.

PS. My mother and my mentors are probably rolling their eyes at me right now - but I made it through the whole book and only cussed once - well twice. Sometimes you have to "give it to the people the way they need it". Jesus will forgive me! That said, don't leave this moment and forget to OYS!

Ask For Help

I listen to and learn from everybody in my life. I really do. Not long ago, I had the opportunity to spend the weekend with my three-year-old Goddaughter. She is so smart and intuitive. At three, she is at the point in childhood development where she is extremely articulate – not necessarily with a filter of appropriateness. She says what she means and means what she says.

I went to help the G-baby get out of the car and she pulled away from me and said "I don't need help, I'm a big girl". Her reaction struck me in such a profound way. We spend all of our formative years rushing to grow up so that we can be Big Girls and Big Boys, who don't need help anymore. When we are young, we think we are invincible – able to do everything on our own. In reality, we receive help from someone, somewhere every day. More importantly, we should never be at a point in life when we are afraid or unwilling to ask for help.

No matter how wise, wealthy, or successful we are, there will always be someone that can come along to enhance our human experience. When they arrive on the scene – don't be too proud to ask for help!

BOOK 3
Becoming

Freedom

Close your eyes for a minute. Go ahead - you won't miss anything. Oh wait, you have to read this before you close your eyes. Ok - read this and then close your eyes. When I think of freedom, I see an angelic being (I see a woman - you might see a man...either way it's all good) with a shimmery, flowing garment gliding in the air as she runs forward. Now I know that in actuality the shimmery garment has the potential to create problems for the angel woman, but follow my vision on this. :) Ok - do you have this image of her or him in your mind running forward freely among the clouds? Imagine how freedom feels, looks, and smells. Now close your eyes, take a deep breath, and keep reading.

The feeling of freedom is so much more rewarding. Despite the fact that we are constantly engaging with the (sometimes) ugliness of life, we all have the ability to walk/run in liberty the same way as this angelic being. Freedom is a mindset - a determination to refuse to allow the weight of the world to entangle you. A decision to pursue a powered life at all costs.

Freedom is not permission to infringe on someone else or disrupt someone else's vibe. Individual freedom may not mean that you have the financial means to be as mobile as you would like or to obtain the things you want. However, your mind is free, your soul is free - so you are free. Are you free within the space you currently occupy? Or are you self-obstructing? Heal your mind and manifest freedom.

I noted earlier in the book, that I hate formality - formality of any kind really. There is something innate in me that just resists formality at all costs. A lot of people really get into that kind of stuff, I don't. I hate dressing up to go to formal events. Shucks – I hate dressing up for work. I hate eating at banquets that require you to know which fork to use at a particular time. I realized last Christmas that I am still not mature enough to sit at the adult table for dinner – way too much formality. I hate teaching or speaking in public with shoes on. I hate titles – my parents named me Ayana and that is sufficient for me. I hate having to sit in a particular place or behave in a certain way because of my credentials. Do you get my drift yet? I despise formality.

Now, don't get me wrong. I conform to formality all of the time and I blend in well. Just know though, that if you ever catch me in a formal situation, check on me because I am probably dying on the inside. I think formality puts restrictions on creative ingenuity and innovation. So where I have the opportunity to eradicate myself from formality, I typically do. I think I always have. I have always pushed the envelope and required an explanation for why things have to be done or handled a certain way. Apologies to anyone that I have ever offended, being unapologetically me. Sorry for the offense, not sorry for being me.

Did you hear the teacher when she said, "Freedom is a mindset"? I did.

I am learning that there are levels to this thing called freedom. I didn't realize how hard I had been trying to conform to other's expectations and requirements for living despite how uncomfortable it made me deep down inside. I started challenging myself to try new things and to seek out small pockets of untapped freedom that I could explore further. On this quest, I remember talking to my mom about this paint and sip event that I was planning to attend with nude male models (don't judge me – I was totally there for the artistic experience). I think I was probably more excited to talk to my mom about the event because she is so conservative and I knew this discussion would make her squirm (like some of you are doing now). As I was talking, I was telling her how invigorated I felt to be able to go where I wanted to go and do the things that I enjoyed without having to worry about what others would think. That is when she gut punched me with her classic mommy truth – grab your tissues. She said, "You haven't changed. This you, the "new" you…is the same you from 10 or 15 years ago. Free, wild, and daring. You were always there though. I am so happy that you are back."

You can only be as free as your mindset is evolved. For many years, I thought I was free. It wasn't until I had the opportunity to live in my own space, on my own again as an adult that I realized that the rules for freedom I had tried to live by for many years were still really restrictive. I had created impenetrable boundaries and social norms that fit the mold of who I thought I should be – not who I knew I was. I didn't recognize how I was getting in my own way of experiencing the joy and goodness that comes along with freedom. When my eyes were opened, I started stumbling upon simple things that I didn't realize could be so freeing. What I appreciate about freedom is that the more liberated you are, the more liberated you can become. There is constant evolution in freedom. Once you free your mind of behaviors, patterns, and rituals that keep you doing the same thing over and over again, you can be open to entertain a new perspective that you may have never considered could be meaningful to you.

A year ago, I drove to Washington DC from Cleveland one night. It was close to midnight when I finally made it back to DC. I was so tired that I literally collapsed on the bed - no sheets, no blanket, just the mattress pad (because my mom taught me that a proper homemaker pulls the bedding off of the bed when you travel and makes it up fresh when you return home). After laying there on the mattress pad for about 10 minutes, I paid attention to the dialogue happening in my mind about the necessity for sheets on the bed. Literally, Me and Me were arguing about the proper way to sleep in the bed as an adult.

Sheets or no sheets?

SHEETS!

Sheets or no sheets?

DEFINITELY SHEETS.

But making up the bed means you have to move and it will take 10-15 minutes to do what needs to be done, so sheets or no sheets????

While all of this back and forth was going on in my mind, Tired Me was sitting there totally dazed and confused. I could not believe that after driving more than 6 hours, that I was seriously having an internal conflict about whether or not I should put sheets on the bed. Uggh! I had had enough. I made the executive decision - no sheets! I really didn't have any energy to put sheets on the bed. Beyond the fact that I didn't have any energy to put sheets on, I realized that I was an audience of one and I could do whatever I wanted to do – nobody could judge me or criticize me for doing what I wanted to do. That is when I realized I was free Free, big free, all of the free!

If you are downright appalled or shaking your head at me for choosing no sheets, you need to live a little. I didn't sleep on a naked mattress pad. I mean, I am a savage, but not that savage. I did not make up the bed fully and waste 10 minutes just to do things the proper way. Instead, I grabbed a flat sheet, threw it over the bed, got my blanket and I passed out.

The next morning when I woke up, I realized all over again that I had slept on the bed without making it up properly. I guess Me & Me were well rested too because the internal conflict tried to pop up again. Once again, I was thrust into the back and forth of what was right in this moment. As the mediator, I sat up, acknowledged the new day and realized that everything around me was ok. I didn't die. All of the bad things that I thought would happen if I slept on an unmade bed, did not happen. I was the winner in this situation. For whatever reason, the quiet rebellion against the norms of my life was so therapeutic. There was something so freeing about just being able to stretch out in the bed and not be concerned about who had an opinion. Maybe that's where the idea to dance like no one is watching came from. When you are walking in your truth, you could care less if people are watching. You follow your own flow and sync with your own vibes. This is freedom!

Since we are in the spirit of sharing, I have another freedom practice that I would like to share. This will probably break some hearts. If nothing else, it will create lots of healthy discussion. So I hate putting toilet paper on the holder! I do not understand the point and I refuse to do it (in my bathroom – I respect the sanctity of other people's bathrooms). Hear me out! We use toilet paper at a high frequency. Typically, within 8 to 10 uses, the roll of toilet paper needs to be replaced. By the time you get the roll on the holder, it's time to replace it. In just the time that I have carved out for writing today, I have been to the restroom at least 8 to 10 times. I am seriously conflicted about putting toilet paper on the toilet paper holder. So I choose not to do it. The only time I put on the toilet paper roll on the holder is when my mom is coming to visit and there is a possibility that she will verbally lash me for not having the toilet paper in the appropriate place. When she leaves, I go right back to doing things my way. This is an example of how rebelling and living in your truth can really help you to walk in freedom.

Take a moment and think about the simple things in your life that create so much internal conflict for you. These things keep you from personally experiencing inner-peace and freedom. Are there things that if you changed them today, your disposition as a person would change? You have to make a decision to pursue peace and to follow freedom at any cost.

When someone asked how I feel about my life these days, I replied that I feel like I am free falling into some space of greatness. I have a new (or renewed) sense of self and this new self-confidence has been affirming to my purpose. I have learned to only go where ALL of me, the WHOLE me, is welcome. All of this transformation, or maybe it was just liberation, helped me to see how I had created invisible boundaries that kept me from really living. More importantly, this caused me to be thoughtful about the ways my perspectives and approach towards life may have caused others to not feel free around me. I only want to project good vibes into the atmosphere. I never want to make anyone feel like they cannot show up authentically. You have the ability to give grace and to empower others to live their truth out loud. Keep your mouth off of other's situation. Even if they share with you what they have been through, who are you to judge? If you don't have anything constructive or positive to add to what someone in your space might be going through, then just keep it to yourself. Do not bind someone up by your words or actions.

My freedom doesn't look like your freedom. My peace doesn't look like your peace. We are surveyors on this journey together, but we are not walking in the same path. We do not have the same shoes and we do not have the same final destination.

Let's be kind to one another. Let's empower one another to walk in truth. Let's encourage one another to walk in liberty every step of the way.

Peace

What you manifest is what you model. I believe there are light walkers, joy walkers, love walkers, and so much more. These people carry and display what they sow into themselves and into those they love. Having these traits or qualities don't make these people perfect, without insecurity, without bad days, or without flaws. However, they understand that giving goes so much farther than harboring hate, resentment, jealousy, or fear. These people choose to pursue the light.

Peace is settling into an intrapersonal space of contentment, stillness, and overall unbotheredness. Peace is achieved in the absence of war – with yourself, others, and the around. War is a strong term to use here, but I want you to think critically about the ways in which you wage war (a literal battle) against yourself, others, and the environments around you, on a regular basis. Many times, our personal battles spill over into our interactions with the people and the world around us. After reading this chapter, it is my hope that you come to a greater understanding of how critical it is to maintain peace, but also so that you can take the necessary steps to defend your peace. Pause for a moment and think about the things that prevent you from living in a state of peace.

I believe I am a peace walker. I sow and reap in peace. I believe that I can bring peace to any moment or situation that is receptive to the power of peace. That last part is the major key - receptive to the power of peace. Everyone and every situation is not receptive to the power of peace.

You have to know how to discern whether or not the moment is receptive to the power of peace. When it is not, you have to make personal peace with that reality and walk away. I didn't just get like this. I had to recognize what was keeping me from achieving a peaceful state. I had to address the peace blockers and create (sometimes uncomfortable) boundaries to protect my peace. And I had to pursue peace at all costs - even in chaotic situations or circumstances. I choose the peaceful path. What brings me peace may not make sense to you or seem peaceful to you, that's ok. That's your truth. Leave me to mine.

Pursuing peace at all costs is making the decision to follow the peaceful path.

I was making a decision with someone not too long ago and the path that they recommended for me to take seemed too disruptive and complicated. I could have acquiesced and done what was asked of me. However, in evaluating the options, I acknowledged that this path had too many unknowns and required me to invest too much energy. The recommended path was not the path that I wanted to take. I had to use that moment as a teaching moment to help this person understand that I will always choose the peaceful path, even if that path puts me in a position to make a greater sacrifice. I am the only one that will protect my peace and intend to do that even if it creates disagreement between me and someone else. If we were abiding together in difference, this would be no issue. There are times when you may have to go out of your way or go the long way to protect your peace.

One of the most common stressors for folks living in the Washington DC metropolitan area is traffic. We literally plan our lives around traffic. Many of us spend an hour or more sitting in traffic, each way to work, five or more days per week. Wasting time sitting in traffic is so frustrating. Rather than toughing it out on the main highways, I have regularly opted to take side streets or what I am considering, the peaceful path (for traffic). Taking the peaceful path adds about 10-15 minutes to my 1/1.5 hour commute. However, the side streets usually allow you to travel at a slightly faster pace, in comparison to the stop and go traffic on the main highways. Additionally, the scenery of driving through various communities is far more peaceful than staring at car bumpers, for over an hour. Do you see how easy that is? Peace is a choice.

When was the last time you chose the peaceful path? Or do you bring chaos and calamity into every door that you walk through? Remaining in a state of peace is an approach to life - a perspective and an attitude. Sometimes you will have to create boundaries to protect yourself from people, places, or things that disrupt your peace. There are some conversations that you may not be able to engage, in an effort to guard your peace. Defending your peace has to be an intrinsic behavior - something that you do because you know how valuable peace is. You have to create and design environments that help you to consistently cultivate peace for yourself and for others.

For example, organizations will usually have a set of guiding principles or best practices. This summary of desired behaviors helps individuals interacting with the organization, to understand expectations for what behaviors are acceptable to the organization. In most cases, this list of guiding principles will help to create the desired organizational environment – where everyone can thrive and work in a psychologically safe space. In an effort to protect your peace, you may have to create a list of guiding principles to help people understand how to interact with you. Having this list of guiding principles makes your expectations very clear to you and the people you interact with on a regular basis.

For example, your list of guiding principles may look a little like this:

Here at Ayana's Safe Space Inc., we are committed to thriving in peace by:

- Staying objective

- Regularly reviving our energy

- Avoiding toxicity

- Immediately stopping anything that kills our vibe

- Choosing the peaceful path

- Speaking to each other with love and truth

Hang your list of guiding principles up in your home or office. You would be surprised how many people will read it, just because it is posted on a wall. Make sure your loved ones are familiar with your guiding principles so that they are not offended if you have to take action to protect your peace. As you connect to new people, talking about your guiding principles should be included in one of your first "getting to know you" conversations. You will have to determine what happens to people that cannot or are not interested in respecting the boundaries around your peace. This list will help you to quickly squash anything that rises up to take you out of your element and disrupt your peace.

Peace looks, feels, and sounds different for everyone. What is peace for me may not be peace for you. However, it is important for you to do the work necessary to be able to say definitively what your requirements for peace are. Peace does not just drop down out of the sky. We have the responsibility to manifest and cultivate peace constantly. Peace is a state of being. Be Peace.

Grace

Grace is such an amazing benefit in life. Call it what you may - blessing, favor, fate, chance, coincidence, destiny, predestination. I see grace as the benefit of receiving something that I do not deserve/could not earn OR not receiving consequence or penalty that I do deserve. Grace is one of those things that as a child I always heard the wise people singing about and thanking God for. Grace (like peace, love, joy, and many other concepts) was amorphous to me. The concept of Grace is not super tangible and it's hard to really understand why it matters – until you do.

I went through a very difficult time where I had to decide if I should sever ties with a group that in some ways raised me. I was indebted to this group and really had come to form my identity through my connection to this group. So the thought of separating from them was a tough one to make. However, I have always been someone who prides myself on maintaining personal integrity. Once that integrity is compromised, I can no longer be associated. Ok so all of that said, I knew I had to make a move. I had to do something to heal the tear in my soul, even if it meant the wound would get deeper temporarily, because I had to walk away.

In the midst all of this going on, I had to find a way to make this transition. I don't even know how I stumbled upon *Grace: More Than We Deserve, Greater Than We Imagine* by Max Lucado, but boy, oh boy am I glad that I did. There are a few books that I can say have revolutionized my life (see my book list in the bonus section at the end of the book). When I say that a book revolutionized my life, what I mean is that the book literally shifted my way of thinking, behaving, and forced me to grow as a human. The way Max tells a story is ABSOLUTELY RIDICULOUS! He is such a gifted author! He has a way of bringing the subtle nuances of a story to life in such a big way. As I was reading the book, there were so many things that I just had never really understood about grace. Reading this book made it apparent to me that grace is something that we do not deserve. Grace also has this really unique quality that protects us from receiving consequences that we may deserve. Grace insulates you so that purpose can be achieved in your life.

Once I had a heightened understanding of what grace really is, it allowed me to see grace more clearly in my day-to-day life. In retrospect, there are so many terrible things that I had done as a child and I know it is nothing but grace that kept me from getting some of the consequences that I should've received. I legitimately know that it was the hand of God that kept me out of real life danger seen and unseen. That's grace - grace is the kind of thing that you don't know has happened, until it has happened.

All of a sudden there you are – trying to figure out how you got into a situation where you have more than you should have – that's grace. Or you might have been in a situation that seemed impossible, but then you look up and you made it through the situation with ease. This is also grace. In many ways, grace is the real MVP. Grace has an impeccable track record of successes – namely keeping us on the appropriate path to reach our destiny. We don't give grace enough credit as the silent partner that makes a major investment in our lives. Thank you grace!

When I was in eighth grade, I was crossing the street with some friends on the way to school one morning. I don't have any recollection of what happened after I stepped down into the crosswalk, but I got hit by a car. My physical body, was struck by a car running a red light. I remember coming to consciousness and my favorite school security guard was there with me. Even though I didn't really understand what was going on, I felt safe enough to be in his arms. Safe enough to (I guess) fall back into unconsciousness.

The next time, I woke up, I was in the hospital and by that time my dad had arrived. I remember him leaning over me and saying "if God kept you alive, he kept you alive for a reason". Looking back on that moment, that's kind of a weird thing to say to a child in the middle of a traumatic event, but I appreciate him speaking life into me and into the situation. I didn't quite understand it then. However, over the years, I have gone back through the limited memories I have of the accident and those two moments of coherence, I can recall vividly. There was no way that I could have understood the role of grace in that moment. Truthfully speaking, I didn't really see grace in this experience, until I started writing this book, 23 years later.

Technically, based on the speed the car was traveling at the time of the accident, I should have died. According to ABC News, 2049 people died from hit and run car accidents in 2016. Now this statistic does not specifically call out the number of people who were hit head on versus those that died driving a car. Either way, the statistic is staggering. The reality is that people die every day from these types of accidents. In reflection, I realized that I probably should have died from the accident! It is without a shadow of doubt that I know that grace (+ mercy and other contributors) were active in that moment keeping my life on track. I hope that through this book and my awareness of grace, that you will become more aware of when you have experienced grace in your life – the benefits and the protections.

In addition to dealing with tragic situations, navigating connectedness with people has definitely been an area where I have seen grace and my ability to give grace, in play. One of the points that Max teaches about in his book, is how we should give grace freely to everyone. I did not understand what it meant to be a giver of grace. I didn't even know that I was qualified enough to give grace to someone else. We all have been empowered to stand in the gap and extend grace to others. We have the power to give someone something they don't deserve. Similarly, we have the power to prevent someone from receiving a punishment or consequence that they should receive. Use this super power wisely.

Giving grace goes along with giving people the freedom to evolve. When you extend grace, you are giving someone permission to make mistakes and feel their way through life in a safe space that allows them the opportunity to learn along the journey. The beautiful thing about being a parent is having the opportunity to teach my kid some of the life skills that she needs to be a solid, balanced person in this world. In the short span of her life, there have been numerous occasions where she did something that she should not have done knowingly.

In these cases, it was up to me whether or not I should extend grace or if she should receive a punishment for her actions. I had to hold her accountable for her behavior or else she will never be prepared to make sound decisions as she grows up. I did this by teaching her how grace works for us and how we have an obligation to extend grace to others. She caught on really quickly and eventually started asking for grace when she knew she was in the wrong and consequences were on the way. The moments where she actually applied the concept of grace are so important to me. I think these situations help her to also understand how to extend grace to others.

I could go on and on about the many ways in which grace has played a major part in insulating me to be able to achieve my highest purpose. I have made so many intentional and glaring mistakes in my life, but I am thankful that God saw the need to give me more grace than I could ever really comprehend.

I hope that you take some time to trace the active role of grace in your life. If you are honest with yourself, you would likely be as astonished as I was to realize that the covert operative, grace, has been in action. I hope that you appreciate the grace in your life, but more importantly, I hope that you start to walk in the steps of a grace giver.

Purpose

Don't you hate looking for something that you know should be there and not being able to find it? For many of us, we are searching for purpose the same way. We do not all qualify to be child prodigies or super geniuses. In fact, most of us are just ordinary people. However, if we get ahold of our purpose, we have the ability to make a significant impact on the world. There is no one person that has had the same impact on all people in the world at the same time. You are not purposed to reach everybody, but there is somebody out there waiting for you to follow the flow of purpose for your life.

In many ways, finding purpose is a journey. As you evolve, parts of your purpose become more and more apparent to you. At some point, you will either hit a peak or have a rock bottom experience that fills your purpose tank and sets you on the path to personal greatness. There is a biblical story attributed to the prophet Jeremiah. In this story, he references his mission/purpose and the fact that the fire of that passion was consuming him from the inside out.

Purpose is like that - if ignored for too long, it will start to consume you. You can't run away from purpose. Well, you can try, but you will not succeed. It is better to pursue purpose - to understand the details of what you are to do, to understand the timing of when you are to do it, and to understand why what you are purposed to do matters. Your purpose may be found in reading to children after school, or cuddling abandoned babies, or writing government policy, or becoming a global influencer. Whatever it is, it matters. Don't let your perception of your purpose deflate your self-worth or slow your speed in working towards your purpose.

Purpose is so much more than what you do as a job every day or the intricacies of who you are as a person. Purpose is more about what you were created to do to make an imprint that enhances the world. That's heavy, but you may never read anything else I write. So I am putting the pressure on now! What you were created to do is big! Treat it that way.

Finding purpose is a pursuit. It doesn't just happen. Walking in purpose is not a mystical thing. You do not arrive at purpose unless you are conscious of it. Purpose is reached for different people at different ages. Just because you are younger or older does not mean that you have missed your purpose. I believe the divine plan for your life has you arriving to the awareness of your purpose at the time that is most beneficial to the universe. Purpose is not even about you. It is about the impact you were created to make on others or to make in the world.

THE ACTUAL PURSUIT

Pursuing purpose is an intentional act on your part to become well acquainted with yourself, first. What are you most passionate about? What gives you the greatest sense of joy and peace? When are you most fulfilled? What are you most troubled by when you see it happening? The responses to these questions can help you find the path that leads to purpose.

I started off bound (bound is so deep lol) in a state of wanting to please everyone and not really paying attention to the clues that had been there all along. I have always been a teacher - from a child I have been a teacher. Teaching my baby dolls, grading homework assignments that my mom brought home from her students, or getting lost in the moment at the chalkboard in one of my dad's empty classrooms at the Civic Center. I love teaching - not for the glory of teaching or being an influencer, but because I LOVE HELPING PEOPLE. I love seeing people take something that I may have shared and making use of it in their everyday life. I love watching people grapple with truth and building from that. It was always there - right under my nose and in my heart, but I didn't pay attention to it.

I feel like I have read every popular book on purpose and have kept my ear to the streets of my heart as I have grown up to be able to identify what it is that I am purposed to do. If you've read the chapters on Journey and Knowledge (p. 13 and 27), you know that I have tried my hands at many things to find my place in purpose. Just because you don't know what you are supposed to be doing, doesn't mean you stop working towards finding that sweet spot. Keep pursuing your passion. Continue to surround yourself with the elements of purpose and eventually, the light will come on. You will be in the right place, at the right time, to step into your own greatness. I promise.

FINDING PURPOSE

When you come to purpose, it is so much harder to do things that are not aligned with your purpose. For example, it's 1 a.m. on a Sunday morning and I have hit a writing stride. Right now, in this moment, typing these words and imagining the hearts and minds that will be reading these words not long from now is so exhilarating. I wish I could shut everything down around me and focus solely on this. It is my pleasure, my passion, and my joy to be investing my time and energy into what I know I am purposed to do - help people pursue powered living. That is how purpose will swell up on you as well. Purpose is unquenchable and will ultimately take the reins of your life.

LIBERTY WRITES STAGES OF PURPOSE

Discovery - This stage can be constant or it can be a fixed amount of time. During this stage, you spend time being introspective - learning about yourself, reflecting on your experiences, and coming to a sense of what your purpose is.

Cultivation - During this time, you get down and dirty with your purpose. Write a purpose statement (personal mission, vision, and value statements also apply). Write the vision and make it plain for you and others. What are the things that you can do to develop yourself to walk freely in your purpose? Do you need to attend a conference, enroll in a certification program, or take a class to help you build skills around your purpose? Do you need to find a mentor or a therapist that can help you work through this stage of forming your purpose? When it is time for you to step out on purpose, you want to have invested enough time in this stage to be fully clothed. Have you ever seen someone leave the house and not be fully dressed? This indicates a lack of preparation or concern. If you are not prepared or concerned enough about yourself, how can you help others?

Building Expertise - I believe that building on your success is the best way to work toward consistently walking in your purpose. It is during this stage that you start to build expertise around your purpose. Branding is such an important practice for you to work at when it pertains to your purpose. Even if you do this work for yourself, understanding your areas of focus helps you to be super intentional about your purpose work. You will be able to decipher opportunities that don't directly align with your purpose and cut them off before you get too invested. Building expertise around purpose helps you to run freely and not pursue purpose haphazardly.

Staying Lit and Running Free - Once you turn purpose up to full throttle, you have to be diligent about maintaining a balance with it. For many of us, purpose can be tremendously rewarding, but terribly exhausting. Be sure to do the things necessary for you to stay mindwhole. Keep perspective and peace. Follow the plan and the path set before you. No matter how dismal things may seem, always keep the light on. There is someone out there famished and waiting for you to nourish them. Stay on purpose.

Finally, and possibly most importantly, you must be OK, not knowing what is next. There are so many affirming messages that remind us that God has a divine order for everything. Stay in the flow of purpose and ride the wave. Pursue every new opportunity with intentionality and remain thankful for every blessing.

BOOK 3
Reflections

Know Your Worth

Shout out to Hip-Hop for gassing us up as a people to see the potential in ourselves, but more importantly, to know our value and what we bring to the table. So boom...I had a personal goal that got derailed because...life happens. Fast forward a few years and I was asked to help someone else do some work that would help them to reach their personal goal, which also happened to be the goal that I had abandoned. As I was helping this other person reach their goal -
a thought came to my mind "think about all of the ways that someone else has benefitted from your brilliance...monetize that." That hit me like a ton of bricks. Here I am just giving away my brilliance and all my purpose driven goodness for someone who probably knows my value, but is exploiting the fact that I do not know (or at the very least charge) my own value. Crazy, right?

So I sat down and calculated my per hour rate. Now of course, your per hour rate based on what you make at your job, may not be nearly what you perceive your worth per hour to be, but at least now you know your base rate. When someone asks you to do something (in business or as a favor), think about the energy and effort you will have to invest to deliver what they are asking you for. Don't just stop there. Calculate the cost for you to deliver. If there is no return on your investment, think carefully about whether or not this is something that you want to do. I started doing this before responding to requests and it significantly changed my way of thinking. Now I understand what it costs me to do something for someone else - in time, money, resources, and energy. This is so important. Set your price and don't be afraid to walk away when someone is unwilling to pay your worth.

A few inspirational personal value quotes, for your reading pleasure:

- "Raise the price, raise it two times"
  – Quavo

- "My success can't be quantified"
  – Beyoncé

- "Know yourself, know your worth"
  – Drake

- "I think I'm getting too much money, everybody mad."
  – O.T. Genasis

- "You hear that? That's the sound of the price going up"
  – Jay-Z

- "I invested in myself that means I'm black owned."
  – Lil' Baby

- "You measure time differently, when you know your cost per hour."
  – Ayana Thomas

- "You say no differently, but respectfully, when you know your cost per hour."
  – Ayana Thomas

- "You invest your energy differently, when you know your cost per hour."
  – Ayana Thomas

Stewardship

Are you a good steward? Not long ago, I was preparing to teach a class on the relationship between purpose and connectedness (Connectedness, p. 55). During my research process, I looked up the definition of stewardship and it blew my mind. I had mostly heard of stewardship in religious settings, associated with financial giving. Yes, giving is necessary in so many different contexts. However, the definition of stewardship includes so much more than merely giving. A steward is someone who helps to carry or bring forth something for someone – similar to a surrogate. Are you prepared to support someone else as they work to reach their full potential?

I am naturally a giver. Most of the time, I give too much. I offer too much. I say too much. I have had to learn boundaries so that I do not dry up my well trying to water someone else's garden. Maintaining boundaries is a very hard chore for true givers. As a giver and good steward, I have learned to give (of my time, of my experience, of my resources) in abundance, so that I can reap in abundance (in peace, in joy, in prosperity, in protection).

When you have the opportunity to be a steward for others, do so, genuinely. Do your part to help someone reach higher and go the distance. We want to see everyone win! Give a little. It won't kill you!

The Power of Choice

Having the ability to choose is such a powerful thing. Making choices is a brain behavior that we often take for granted. Similar to memory making, our brain makes choices constantly throughout the day that we are not always aware of. Do I walk the stairs or take the elevator? Do I pour my beverage in a cup or do I drink from a straw? Do I speak my mind or do I keep my mouth shut? These are all choices that we make. Don't get me wrong, there are far more complicated choices that we make on a daily basis. I used these examples to illustrate the frequency at which we make decisions that we give little attention to - they just come naturally. I have two points that I want to make on choice (and now that I am thinking out loud, this probably should have been a whole chapter - maybe a special feature for *Life Light: Part Deux*).

Back to my two thoughts - here goes:

Use the wisdom that you have to make the best choices that you can. As you grow in wisdom, you will make better choices. Do not beat yourself up for poor choices that you have made now or in your past. At the same time, don't get stuck on stupid or wallow in self-pity. Learn from the choices you've made, count the costs/weigh all of the options in future decisions and keep pressing on.

My second thought is this - many times folks get decision paralysis because there is fear associated with the risk of the choices you have to make. Rather than getting stuck in fear, see yourself in power or empowered to make a choice. As a strong, smart, and successful person (manifest these ideas even if you are not quite there), you have the power to make a choice that can enhance your now and next. What will you choose?

Clarity

Oh to be clear – to be seen clearly, to be heard clearly, and to see clearly. Clarity has two primary definitions: 1) to be coherent and intelligible and 2) to be transparent. When I think about clarity, I think about how uncomfortable it can be driving through a patch of fog. When you cannot see where you are going, your body has so many different reactions. As soon as the fog breaks, all of the anxiety and angst eases. Wouldn't it be nice if all of our days were totally clear?

Unfortunately, the way life works, we know that there will be cloudy days and days where the fog is so thick, that we don't feel like we can move forward. Some of us may even get stuck in this place for more than a few days, because we cannot function in the absence of clarity. I hope that *Life Light* has helped you develop a greater sense of clarity on the various topics included in the book. I hope that if you don't have clarity that you will do the work necessary to gain clarity – so that you can be fully present with yourself, others and the around. I also hope that you are able to use the strategies provided in this book to clear out the things in your life that may prevent you being able to see your purpose in a transparent way – no fog.

Every year, I complete a clarity cleanse to help me prepare for the year to come. It is a seven day cleanse that forces me to withdraw myself from life's unnecessary distractions (namely social media and Netflix binge watching), so that I can seek direction. Sometimes the circumstances of life will not allow you to physically separate yourself from home or work to get the direction that you need in life. The clarity cleanse is designed to help you tap into your divine source to obtain guidance that helps you reach towards your greatness. The clarity cleanse helps you to focus on reflection - asking yourself the tough questions and dealing with the tough realities. More importantly, the clarity cleanse will help you come to solutions that will help you to walk clearly towards your future.

I hope that you are clear on my intentions for you to reach your highest potential. More importantly, it is my hope that you succeed there. Be open to evolution and follow peace with every step.

Details for the Liberty Writes Clarity Cleanse are included in *Life Light: The Workbook.*

Cultivating

I love the concept of cultivating. I use this word a lot in the business world to sound smart. Cultivating implies digging in (with your hands) and raising something from seed to fruit. A little different from manifesting, cultivating is the dirty work required to bring things (ideas, vision, etc.) to reality. There are times when manifesting is not enough. You will have to lean in and get some sweat on your brow. You may have to get a little dirt under your fingernails to reach your end goal. Don't stop now. Dig in and do the dirty work. Your future self will be very grateful that you did!

Closing Reflection

Wow!

Momma, I made it!

Whew! Wow!

OMG!

I feel all of this at the same time. Writing this book has been on the forefront of my heart and mind for quite some time. To see it through to fruition feels so amazing. I have been vulnerable, transparent, and honest. I hope that bearing my soul and the light of it, helps you to find your light, walk in the light, and keep the light on for someone coming behind you. Just because you have finished reading this book does not mean that your work is done. If you did not use the workbook in tandem with your reading, I would highly suggest that you invest your time to do some additional digging. Pursuing your best self is not a quick work – it is something that you must master over time.

Thank you for going on this journey with me. I hope that there is an opportunity for our paths to cross so that I can learn more about how this book has helped you pursue powered living as your best self!

Peace and Liberty!

BONUS Section

LIBERTY WRITES WORD BANK:

I enhanced or created new definitions for the terms included in the Word Bank.

Evolve – follow the free flow of development over time, as you learn from and interact with yourself, your tribe, and the world around you.

Freedom – making a conscious decision to live untangled from self-imposed or socially imposed expectations that confine your greatness

Trauma – the imprint left on a person (physical, emotional, psychological, or spiritual) as a result of an intensely stressful experience, moment, or circumstance.

Liberty Writes 24-Second Rule™ – anytime you need to take a break, reset, or reframe your thoughts. Close your eyes and take three deep breaths.

Mindfulness – present awareness of self, others, and the around (that is anything and everything around you)

Mindwholeness – the idea that the mind must be whole in order for you to have a proper relationship with yourself, others and the around

Peace – settling into an intrapersonal space of contentment, stillness, and overall unbotheredness

Perspective – happens when your past experiences collide with your present reality

READS THAT HAVE REVOLUTIONIZED MY LIFE:

1. *The Coldest Winter Ever* by Sister Souljah

2. *Single, Married, Separated, and Life After Divorce* by Miles Monroe

3. *Grace: More Than We Deserve, Greater Than We Imagine* by Max Lucado

4. *The Purpose Driven Life* by Rick Warren

5. *The Role of Meaning and Emotion in Learning* by Pat Wolfe

6. *Experience, Consciousness, and Learning: Implications for Instruction* by Barry Sheckley and Sandy Bell

7. *A Moment of Silence: Midnight III* by Sister Souljah

8. *Year of Yes: How to Dance It Out, Stand in the Sun, and Be Your Own Person* by Shonda Rhimes

9. *Battlefield of the Mind: Winning the Battle in Your Mind* by Joyce Meyer

10. *The Five Love Languages: How to Express Heartfelt Commitment to Your Mate* by Gary Chapman

11. *Me and My Big Mouth: Your Answer is Right Under Your Nose* by Joyce Meyer

12. *Blink* by Malcolm Gladwell

13. *A Second Chance: Grace for the Broken* by Keith Battle

14. *The Five Love Languages of Children* by Gary Chapman and D. Ross Campbell

15. *Me, Myself, and I Am* by Matthew Peters

16. *The Hard Questions: 100 Essential Questions to Ask Before You Say "I Do"* by Susan Piver

17. *Biblical Mathematics: Keys to Scripture Numerics* by Ed. F. Vallowe

THOMAS MODEL OF INDIVIDUAL LEARNING

The Thomas Model of Individual Learning provides a systematic structure for measuring the effectiveness of information/knowledge transfer between teacher and student. This process of learning can be observed in simple tasks like learning how to tie a pair of shoes to learning complex STEM systems. Ultimately, teachers should aspire to have their students develop into teachers. In a traditional classroom, raising up students to be teachers enhances the peer-to-peer synergy and can increase the rate of learning.

MASTERY

TEACHING

When a student is able to successfully guide another student through this model, they have reached the mastery level of learning, which is teaching. Teachers are able to articulate the same information they were taught at base level, with an easiness and ability to adapt the information for various learning styles. Teachers are able to mesh complex concepts and return them to students in a comprehensible manner. Teachers remember their process of learning and desire to bring out the best in their students. They will be patient and draw from their learning experience to design an optimal learning environment for their students.

SUCCESSFUL APPLICATION

Reaching this level of learning is to be celebrated! After a period of repetition with the information, a student is able to successfully apply what they have learned without intervention from the teacher and without error. It was important to include this level of learning because so many learners try to advance from application to teaching without successfully applying what they have learned, over time. It is crucial that students invest the time at this level of learning, to master the intricacies of the information they are toiling with, so that they can function liberally at the highest level of learning.

APPLICATION

The goal of teaching should be to help students develop independence with the information you are sharing. At the application level, students have the ability to manipulate the information without the guidance of the teacher. In application, the student works through continued practice with the information. At this level, mistakes are made and the student is able to regroup and develop through trial and error..

UNDERSTANDING

Aha!...is usually what teachers hear at this level of learning. Students have developed to the level of understanding, when they are able to grasp the detail of the information that you have shared with them. For processes, students can at least, articulate the outcome or the goal of the learning exercise. In other fact based information sharing, students may be able to start piecing related concepts together.

PERCEIVING

Perceiving is the base level of learning. At this level, students come into contact with new information.Depending on the setting and the context, students may have the opportunity to interact with the information by problem solving or logic building. Learning for many people ceases at the perceiving level. This may be the case because students do not have the capacity to make meaning of the new information. This can also happen when the reinforcement necessary to advance to the higher levels of learning is absent.

INFORMATION TRANSFER

THOMAS MODEL ON
TEACHER/STUDENT DUALITY

The Thomas Model on Teacher/Student Duality focuses on the interrelationship between the role of the teacher and the student. Equal action must be taken in order for synergy to be cultivated between the teacher and the student.

The model also demonstrates how an individual can traverse the boundaries between teacher and student. There are times when a teacher must be available to receive and process information as a student. Likewise, there are times when a student takes on the role of an instructor in a teaching moment.

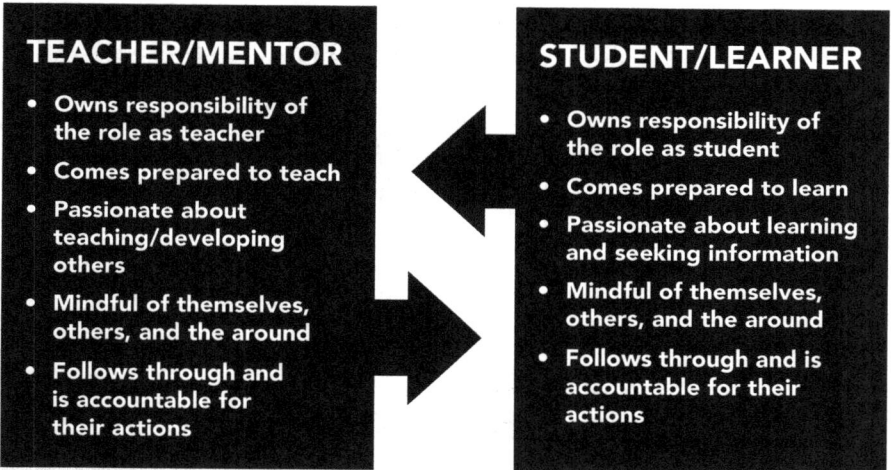

TEACHER/MENTOR

- Owns responsibility of the role as teacher
- Comes prepared to teach
- Passionate about teaching/developing others
- Mindful of themselves, others, and the around
- Follows through and is accountable for their actions

STUDENT/LEARNER

- Owns responsibility of the role as student
- Comes prepared to learn
- Passionate about learning and seeking information
- Mindful of themselves, others, and the around
- Follows through and is accountable for their actions

Teachers should exhibit these behaviors when they are preparing to SHARE information with their students (Teacher/Student):

- Become a student of the material first to learn as much as you can - this can include conducting additional research and pulling in additional resources to support the learning moment.
- Identify key lessons to share with your students.
- Consistently listen to your presentation as a student, when you are preparing to teach and as you deliver the content.

Teachers usually exhibit these behaviors when they have the opportunity to LEARN (Student/Teacher):

- Teachers should remove their teacher hat and become a sponge to the material being presented.
- Teachers can be critical of other teachers who are not prepared for the teaching moment.
- Teachers are consistently thinking of ways that they would teach the lesson.

WORKS CITED OR REFERENCED FOR WRITING PURPOSES:

Consistently Lit:

- Cube, I. (Producer) & Raboy, M. (Director). (2002). Friday After Next. United States: New Line Cinema.

- Hahn, D. (Producer) & Allers, R., Minkoff, R. (Directors). (1994). The Lion King. United States: Walt Disney Pictures.

Journey/Evolution:

- van der Kolk, B. (2014). The Body Keeps The Score: Brain, Mind, and Body in the Healing of Trauma, New York: Penguin Books.

Trauma:

- Huncho Dreams [Recorded by Quavo]. Quavo Huncho [Studio Album]. Los Angeles, CA: Capital Records.

Mindwholeness:

- Triggered [Recorded by Jhene Aiko]. Single [Digital Download]. New York City, NY: Def Jam Recordings.

- Lomas, T. (2016, March). Where Does the Word Mindfulness Come From? Retrieved from https://www.psychologytoday. com/us/blog/mindfulness-wellbeing/201603/where-does-the-word-mindfulness-come

- Bell, S., Sheckley, B. (2006). Experience, Consciousness, and Learning: Implications for Instruction. New Directions for Adult and Continuing Education (43-53). San Francisco: Jossey Bass.

- Wolfe, P. (2006). The Role of Meaning and Emotion in Learning. New Directions for Adult and Continuing Education (35-41). San Francisco: Jossey Bass.

WORKS CITED OR REFERENCED FOR WRITING PURPOSES:

Own Your Shit

- Walker, M. (2017). Quotes retrieved from various videos retrieved from https://www.youtube.com/channel/ UCXqcrtyJryKeb37iDrLphmw

Grace

- Lucado, M. (2014). Grace: More Than We Deserve, Greater Than We Imagine. City, State: Thomas Nelson Publishers.

- Siu, B. (2018, April). Hit-and-Run Deaths at All-Time High, New AAA Study Says. Retrieved from https://abcnews. go.com › hit-run-deaths-time-high-aaa-study › story

Know Your Worth

- Huncho Dreams [Recorded by Quavo]. Quavo Huncho [Studio Album]. Los Angeles, CA: Capital Records.

- Top Off [Recorded by DJ Khaled, Jay-Z, Future, and B]. Father of Ashad [Studio Album]. Los Angeles, CA: Epic Records.

- 0 to 100/The Catch Up [Recorded by Drake]. Single [Studio Recording]. New Orleans, LA: Young Money

- Everybody Mad [Recorded by O.T. Genasis]. Single [Digital Download]. Brooklyn, NY: Conglomerate.

- Mood4EVA [Recorded by Beyonce, Jay-Z, Childish Gambino, Oumou Sangare]. The Lion King: The Gift [Studio Album]. New York City, New York: Parkwood.

- Back On [Recorded by Lil' Baby]. Quality Control: Control The Streets, Vol. 2 [Studio Album]. Atlanta, GA: Quality Control.

Meet the Author

Ayana Thomas has demonstrated success in people development as an organizational consultant and counselor in federal government, higher education, private sector, and religious organizations.

Her goal is to help people reach and then succeed at their highest potential. Whether it's influencing people in a 1-1 setting or teaching a group, Ayana believes that we are all purposed to do great things. Ayana founded Liberty Writes, LLC. and is tapping into her gift as an Author to help people all over the world pursue powered living.

For upcoming appearances and books, visit ayanathomas.com.

Liberty Writes

**BUILDING PEOPLE
PURSUING POWERED LIVING**

LIBERTY WRITES IS HERE TO HELP YOU!

Liberty Writes is a people development brand that focuses on building the whole person. The brand offers career, family, and organizational development services.

Visit ayanathomas.com to learn more!

CPSIA information can be obtained
at www.ICGtesting.com
Printed in the USA
LVHW011913200622
721665LV00007B/67

9 780578 610429